MW00586211

Broken and Beautiful: The greatest beauty comes from our deepest pain

By Amber Stewart

Published by Amber Stewart, 2020.

While every precaution has been taken in the preparation of this book, the publisher assumes no responsibility for errors or omissions, or for damages resulting from the use of the information contained herein.

BROKEN AND BEAUTIFUL: THE GREATEST BEAUTY COMES FROM OUR DEEPEST PAIN

First edition. November 27, 2020.

Written by Amber Stewart.

Table of Contents

Dedication

I dedicate this book first to my Lord Jesus Christ, without whom I am nothing. Second, to my family who believe in me and push me to be my best. I also dedicate this book to Vicki Price Gruver, who was my AP English teacher in high school and said she always wanted a book dedicated to her. I hope this makes you smile.

Lastly, for anyone out there living with Spinal Muscular Atrophy, ALS, Muscular Dystrophy, or other diseases that rob you of your strength, this book is for you. You are not alone. You are not a mistake or an inconvenience to this world. You are loved more than you will ever imagine by the same God who knew that this crazy world needed you in it. You have a special purpose, and you matter. Please don't give up. Blessings always await those who persevere. The strongest people are those who clawed their way through Hell to find the mountain that was meant for them. Sometimes it feels like it never ends and, you know, it might not. That is why God made us warriors for Him and if you really know Him, I promise, life is better.

I pray that this book will serve as a banner of hope for all who read it.

Introduction

Once upon a time... No, that will not work. How about, there once lived a girl...? That doesn't sound right either. See, this is not your typical fairytale or bedtime story; there are no wizards or vampires, even though that would be interesting. However, this is my story; my life, and how what man said was impossible, God made possible. In case you are still a little lost, I, Amber Stewart, am about to take you through my crazy life. It is one unlike any other you have read – one filled with divine power. This is a love story unlike any you have heard: about how the most powerful love of the God of the universe changed my life forever. My story is emotional, raw, and 100% me. It is filled with highs and lows and peace that passes all understanding. Now that that is out of the way, let us move on. My life has been quite a rollercoaster ride, so hold on tight and let us begin.

Chapter 1

Imagine the pain of having established doctors sit you and your spouse in an empty room to tell you that your third child will not live to be two years old. I probably should have mentioned before that your firstborn went to be with the Lord at six months old. OK, being hypothetical is not exactly working for me so let's try that again...

My parents, Matthew and Alice Stewart were married three weeks after my mom turned eighteen. Matthew built a rancher home in Port Deposit, Maryland, and the newlyweds moved in right away in hopes of starting a family. About two years later, on September 16, 1987, my older sister Lindsey was born. However, shortly after my sister came into this world, everyone knew she was not a healthy baby girl. She was diagnosed with a genetic disease called Spinal Muscular Atrophy, which is the number one genetic killer of kids under the age of 2. Since you probably have no clue what SMA is, I'll give you the basics: everyone has nerve endings attached to their spinal cord and usually your brain sends impulses or commands down your spinal cord to the motor neurons, which then sends the impulses to your muscles, and that's how you move. People that suffer from SMA are not mentally handicapped or slow, but when their brains send impulses down to their muscles to move, the motor neurons get lost traveling from the brain to the muscles. Those who suffer from this disease are lacking an important protein that allows our muscles to react on command, and that protein is produced by a gene known as SMN1. That gene is missing altogether and thus so is the needed protein. It's easier if you think of it as a battery plugged into an electrical outlet, but it is not plugged in all the way. This disease is often described as ALS in infants. Approximately one out of every 6,000 babies are diagnosed with SMA, and out of those diagnosed only 50% survive. Both parents have to be carriers of the disease, and even then, their kids only have a 25% chance of getting SMA. The disease affects ones' mobility, breathing, and swallowing, which can all be less or more severe depending on what type of Spinal Muscular Atrophy one has. Lindsey was diagnosed with type one, also known as Werdnig-Hoffman Disease, which is the most severe SMA type out of four. My parents loved and cared for my sister for six months, then she left this world and did not suffer anymore. I do not think I will ever be able to understand the pain that my parents felt the following two years after they buried Lindsey Amber Stewart. After they were starting to get past their grief, my mom found out she was pregnant with my brother, Matt, who was born on December 30, 1988. Matt Joseph Stewart, or "Bubba" as I call him, was born healthy and of course had Mom and Dad's undivided attention. After my parents lost my sister, they didn't want to let Matt out of their sight for fear that something may happen to him. Two years later I was born on January 31, 1991, and I was healthy as well, or so it seemed. When I was around five months old though, I stopped wiggling and rolling around all of the sudden, and Mom knew something wasn't quite right. She took me to the hospital and the doctors simply thought she was paranoid that I would be like my sister; so they tried in their blind ignorance to pat her head and send her off like a good little girl, assuring her all the while that I was fine. The professionals probably were not mothers though, because they could not understand that feeling a mom has when she knows her baby is sick. Mom and Dad then took me to another doctor who did a test where they shock your muscles and see if they respond. They did not respond, which confirmed everyone's worst fear: I had Spinal Muscular Atrophy – type 1 - just like my sister.

Chapter 2

Even though my parents had already been through it with the death of their baby girl, they eventually started moving on. My big brother helped the whole process, and although they had had some major trials in their first few years of marriage, my family knew that God was still on His throne and their lives were starting to get back in order. Then my doctors dropped the bomb that I had Werdnig-Hoffman Disease, and wouldn't live to be 2. A few statistics about those diagnosed with Type 1: 50% survive the first year, and out of those only 10% live past two years. My parents knew the doctors knew what they were talking about. When people have kids, it is understood that all they want is for their babies to be happy and healthy. I was not healthy, that is for sure; but I was happy! So, my family took me, death date and all, home to love me and make the most out of every day they had with me.

Now the first six years of my life were a little blurry, but I will try my best to give you every detail - after all, those were the craziest years of my life. When I was around 18 months old, Alfred I. DuPont Children's Hospital became my second home. I was hospitalized approximately every two weeks until I was 3, usually with pneumonia. Most children are terrified at the mere thought spending the majority of your childhood in a hospital; I on the other hand actually got homesick for the hospital as I got older and spent less time there. By the time I was 5 I knew almost every nurse on the PICU unit, and it is a large unit. Whenever I was hospitalized, I usually had one respiratory therapist who was assigned specifically to care for me around the clock. Every few hours I required intense chest percussions on all left, right, front and back sections, as well as breathing treatments. My nickname was "Baby Squeezy" because my parents literally had to squeeze me in order to help me cough up secretions and the RTs couldn't do the same for fear that they would hurt me. Nevertheless, my family and I grew quite close to the hospital staff and tried to make the most of our time there. They had a playroom that all the patients could go in and make crafts or play games, and whenever I was able to get up, I loved to go there and paint things. Perhaps it was because I was so young, but I never got angry that I was always in the hospital outliving every expiration date the doctors set for me while being poked, prodded, and beaten on around the clock. God's presence was more real to me from the time I was an infant than most people acknowledge in a lifetime.

I had my first medical procedure done when I was a little over 2 years old. I had severe reflux at the time, so they gave me a G-tube: a small tube about the size of a quarter that goes in your stomach that acts as another port that you can get all your food and nutrition through. After the doctors put it in, they thought that would be the end of my reflux problems. They were wrong. I threw up everything I ate and drank, and I was soon starving to death. I went back to the hospital, of course, and the doctors then put in a J-tube: same tube in another place. That didn't work either, and I needed something called a Nissen fundoplication, which is a surgery where they actually wrap the upper part of your stomach around your esophagus, essentially making it impossible for you to throw up. The bad part was that I was not strong or healthy enough to have surgery, and if they tried, I would surely die on the table... So, we were back to the whole starving to death situation.

Chapter 3

Let's see, where was I? Oh, right, I was dying. My doctors had already done procedures to put in a G-tube and when that did not work, they put in a J-tube, but I still could not keep anything down. I had two options according to the doctors: starve to death or die on the operating table because I was too weak. So, what do you do when the ground under you seems to be shattering? You pray. We were completely incapable of changing the situation on our own, so my family placed all their worries and fears in the hands of God and trusted that He would make a way.

When you are in the hospital, however short you may be there, you are probably aware that the bills pile up pretty quick. I was living in the hospital at the time and Mom never left my side, not even for ten minutes; so Dad ended up working every day all day and crashing at the Ronald McDonald House while my brother lived with my grandparents the majority of the time. One night when Dad was working and Bubba was with our Ma-ma and Pa-pa, Mom was beside my bed asking God to tell her what I needed to survive. Have you ever had a moment where it is as if God is sitting right beside you because you can hear His voice so clear? Well, my mom had a moment like that while she was praying; plain as day, God told her I needed TPN. The crazy part was that she did not even know what TPN was; it did not matter though, because Mom knew that was what I needed. She called my dad and told him the great news, and even though he had no clue what TPN was himself, he knew I needed it and supported my mom, Alice. My dad came to the hospital as soon as he could, and they both called my doctors into my room and told them I needed TPN. The "professional" doctors practically laughed in my parents' faces, saying that it would damage my liver and kill me. I was going to die anyway, and my parents knew I needed it, so Dad told them if they did not give me TPN they would take me to another hospital where they would. In December of '93, they did surgery to give me a Central Line which is required to administer TPN. A Central Line is like an IV, but instead of going into your veins, it goes in one of your arteries and can stay in for years. After the Central Line was placed, they started giving me TPN, or Total Parenteral Nutrition, which is a liquid mixture of vitamins and nutrients. However, it does not feed your stomach, it feeds your blood. Either way, though, it fed me, and I could keep it down. I went home with the Central Line and TPN without any nursing. What you do not understand is how easy it is to get infections which are very dangerous. You have to keep everything sterile, and even then, infection is possible. I had my Central Line for 18 months without one infection. That was June of 1994, and I was strong enough to get a fundoplication. You still think there isn't a God?

Chapter 4

When I was four years old, I had to have a spinal fusion. A spinal fusion is a surgery for people with severe scoliosis where doctors put a metal rod in your back. Scoliosis is common with people that have SMA, and sometimes they can just wear a back brace. However, my spine was so curved that it was crushing my lungs and without the surgery I would die. I was in the hospital for two weeks recovering.

I had to have my tonsils taken out in that same year. What should have a simple procedure was anything but that. If you have never had a tonsillectomy you probably are not aware that after they take out your tonsils, they cauterize your mouth to prevent bleeding. Cauterization is where doctors actually burn the blood vessels in your mouth. It usually works for everyone, but what we soon found out was that I do not clot at all. I was losing so much blood that they had to put me to sleep again and re-cauterize my mouth, which they never have to do. It worked though because I finally stopped bleeding.

The next three years went by pretty smooth; I was homeschooled by my mom kindergarten and first grade. My dad, Matthew, sang in a southern gospel quartet that was started at our church. My buddies and adopted family: Delmer and Ronny Duvall, Chucky Boyd, and Phil Fisher also sang with Dad in The Nottingham Four. The group was asked to sing at a church in North Carolina, and Mom wanted to go with them. She had never left me before, but I had been doing so well the past few years, so my grandparents on both sides of my family came over to take care of Bubba and me. My parents left on a Friday night and got one day of peace before all hell broke loose.

Chapter 5

Have you ever gone unconscious? I am assuming not, so I will try to describe the whole blackout experience. Imagine someone pressing the fast forward button on your life for what feels like hours instead of seconds. Everyone seems to be moving at speaking at supersonic speeds, then it's all opposite. They all suddenly look like zombies because they are reacting so slowly, even though only seconds have passed. Then when they finally do reach you and keep asking if you can hear them, you can't say anything. Everything goes black after that. Maybe it's not the same for everyone, but that is exactly how I remember it on that Sunday morning. We were all in the kitchen, and my grandma on Mom's side was making breakfast for us all; everybody was having a great morning. That is, until I lost consciousness. I remember right before I completely blacked out, all my grandparents hovered around me, shouting things like "can you hear me, Amber?", "She's turning blue!", "Someone call an ambulance!"…

I completely lost consciousness after that. My grandpa on my mom's side got me up on the kitchen table and gave me CPR for an hour until the ambulance got there. While he was doing CPR, Dad's mom, Ma-ma, and my big brother Matt were in another room on their knees praying for me. According to my grandma, I was pretty popular because we drew a big crowd. My second father figure, Kenny Shackelford, and the associate pastor at Matt's school, Dennis Watson, came to the house, broke up the crowd, got beside me and prayed while my Pop-pop was still doing CPR. Don't tell me prayer does not work - I still had a pulse when the EMS got there, and they rushed me to Havre De Grace Memorial Hospital. Once I got there, they tried to stabilize me and intubate me. Intubation is where doctors stick a tube down your throat, past your vocal cords, into your trach, and actually pump air into your lungs with something called an ambu bag. However, they could not get an airway established because I was unable to open my mouth far enough for anyone to intubate me, and I did not have any veins to get an IV started. So, for the next four hours or so, emergency paramedics bagged me as a last resort to keep air in me somehow. Sometime while all the chaos in Maryland was going on, my parents found out that I was in critical condition. Dad's group was singing at a church in NC if you remember. Try to imagine what was going through their heads when in the middle of the church service, they witnessed state troopers storming in, up to the front of the church to take them aside and inform them of what was going on. Needless to say, they hopped a flight immediately. Meanwhile, while Mom and Dad were in Wilmington, NC waiting to hop on a jet to come back home and check on me, my primary physician, Dr. McCluskey, was flying from DuPont to the small town of Havre De Grace, Maryland, to attempt like he had dozens of times before to get a more stabilized airway so I could be air lifted to DuPont. Once he arrived, though, they had already gotten an airway route established. After I was somewhat stable, I was air lifted to A.I. DuPont Children's Hospital, which was about an hour away by car. Upon arrival, doctors tried to stabilize me, at least until my parents could get there and discuss my fragile condition and decide where to go from there.

Chapter 6

By the time my parents flew home, most of the chaos was past us. I stayed in the hospital for about a week while dealing with the horrifying episodes of my failing to breathe every time I sat up. When all other options had failed, my mother and father gave the physicians permission to place a tracheotomy, or trach, in me. A trach is a small tube that goes right under your throat in your airway, and people have easy access to it for all your respiratory needs such as ventilating, treatments, and suctioning. Doctors that specialize in SMA make parents paranoid of letting their children get trachs because they think it's the beginning of the end; but ever since I got my trach, I have been healthier than before it was placed. The days following my getting trached consisted of doctors monitoring me while teaching my family, including my 9-year-old brother, everything they could possibly know about taking care of a trach. Matthew, Alice, and Matt had to practice suctioning and changing a trach and get everything down pat before I was able to leave the hospital. After all that was over, everything was smooth sailing for the most part. I was still in and out of A.I. DuPont Children's Hospital for check-ups and such, but nothing too major.

I know you have not gotten too far in this book, but with all that I have already told you about me, can you honestly say God had no part in any of that? That I was just lucky? Let us get real here - it would have taken all the luck on earth just to get me to age 5. That was not luck, but was providence of a loving, gracious, almighty God. All through my childhood I knew about the plan of salvation: how thousands of years ago God knew that unless His only, beloved, perfect son came to earth in the form of a man and bridged the gap between Heaven and earth, every person would die in sin without the promise of Heaven. I knew John 3:16 which says, "For God so loved the world that He gave His only begotten son; that whosoever believeth in Him should not perish, but have everlasting life." Even though I knew all this, I had not asked Him into my heart, until one summer night in 1999. Of all the bizarre ways for God to reveal Himself to me, He chose to do so through a dream. I dreamt I was in the same position Christ was in, on the cross; but I was trying to get myself to Heaven. Right before I was about step up to the cross, Christ took my place so I would not have to suffer. Strange, I know, but God works in mysterious ways. We had company over that day and Mom and Dad wanted to wait until everyone had gone home so they could make sure I really understand how to be saved. So, I waited, and waited, and although it seemed like the longest day ever, that night on our living room couch I asked Jesus Christ into my heart. Some people think you have to know the time and day you got saved or it doesn't count. Those people are mistaken. The fact is I nailed down my salvation and God sealed my destiny forever. I think the Christian group Newsong says it best in one of their songs: "when you believe He's all you need, that will be your defining moment. As you live your life walking in His life, trusting Him completely, that will be your defining moment." It was hard when I was younger to understand why Christ would die for someone like me, then it hit me: instead of Christ thinking about all the times I would reject Him and continually return to a life of sin, I believe with all my heart that right before His crucifixion He was thinking of why He was dying for everyone on earth and specific people came to His mind. I bet I was one of those people and He thought something like this: "I have to finish this because in 1991, a little girl named Amber Kristen Stewart is going to be afflicted with a disease because of sin. If I do not finish this and fulfill my promise that I would rise again, Amber isn't going to be able to survive on her own." Maybe that sounds ridiculously conceited, that I actually believe the son of God was thinking of me moments before He was placed on a cross to die. Guess what else I believe without a doubt? He was thinking of you too; how even though you have and will make mistakes and even make a total wreck out of your life, Christ will forgive you and make you one of His children if you just ask.

Chapter 7

At the age of seven, my family presented me with an extremely exciting new opportunity: summer camp. In the tiny town of Millville, PA, lies one of the most amazing camps ever created, known as Camp Victory. This camp actually offers a multitude of individual camps that are geared toward special needs children, from Autistic Camp to Camp Little People. The camp that I began going to that first year is called PA Vent Camp. Doctors, nurses, respiratory therapists, and people just wanting to help all volunteer their time to welcome at least thirty special-needs kids and teenagers with trachs and ventilators or bipaps to a week they will never forget. The campers each have one nurse and one aid that is with them from sunup to sundown for all five days and another nurse that cares for them at night. What does that mean? No parents allowed. You drop your child off, get them settled in, and leave. Four days later pick them up and hear all the stories they have to share about the amazing adventures they had and the friends they made – and the silence when they fall asleep exhausted from the long week – on the way home.

While the children that come to PA Vent Camp have varying serious medical conditions, they are treated like any "normal" child while at camp. They have the chance to go rock climbing, zip lining, swimming, fishing, boating, and do many other activities they otherwise would never be able to do had it not been for such an extraordinary camp. I hesitantly but excitedly jumped at the chance, and while my first year there was difficult being away from my family, I went back every year since and have made many lifelong friends in doing so. So many memories accompany each of my camp visits; like the time the girls trashed the boy's cabin, which was my idea, and they retaliated by unleashing a cooler full of frogs in my cabin. Or the time that I was one of the firsts to go up the rock wall on a ventilator, and my awesome nurse friend, Mike, climbed the wall with me with my vent strapped to his back the whole time. Or every year when we all at some point had an epic water gun battle and ended up soaked the rest of the day. I still attend a new adult Vent Camp every year, and I would not miss out on this experience for anything.

When you go to camp the first time, what you do not realize is that everyone becomes a family rather quickly. We've had amazing times together and even have lost loved ones together. The Bible talks of how we are to bear one another's burdens, and everyone at camp lives this out. The camp is not strictly a "Christian" camp, but you can see God when you see so many people caring for completely handicapped children without asking for anything else in return. You see Jesus through the eyes of a disabled child who still chooses to love life in spite of their challenges. And once campers and even volunteers get home from camp, most are already counting down the days until they get to visit once again. Because when we are all together, it feels like home.

Chapter 8

Near the Fall of '99, Mom asked if I wanted to go to the school my brother went to, Lighthouse Christian Academy. Of course, I jumped at the chance, but I am sure you can imagine my parents' worries: that I'd be made fun of, that something would happen to me medically such as getting sick more often… I didn't care about any of that stuff though, I was excited. So, I started the second grade that fall with all the other kids and fell into the swing of things pretty fast. I believe there were around nine other kids in my class; seven of whom were boys. The other two girls were nice, but the boys were less dramatic and soon became my brothers. I was of course only interested with being with my friends, but I did do well in the academic part of school. I guess you could say I had a fairly normal childhood, aside from routine hospital visits and whenever I got sick. As far as school went, I was not bullied at all; in fact, there was a few times I cornered friends and told them I'd let them out for five bucks! About that time my mom or nurse would jerk me back in line, but that was pretty much as bad as I got as a kid. That, and the time I stole two pieces of chalk in the third grade, which I returned the next day. Hypothetically though, if I didn't stand up for myself and others picked on me, I bet my buddies would have jumped all over them; they had my back. Especially this one time in the third grade when we were putting on a play and my teacher would not let me be in it because of my speech problem. To be honest, I am somewhat hard to understand if you are not around me much, however this was an elementary school production, and I was devastated that everyone but me was in it. Most of my classmates then dropped out of the play until our teacher gave me a role, which she did.

Looking back on the three years I attended LCA, I realize how much fun I had there: pirate days and pilgrim days where we got to dress up and do things they did back then, playing recess with my best friends, and doing tons of other stuff that ended all too soon.

Chapter 9

I was 11 years old and life as I knew it was pretty great; I was exceling in grade school, I had lots of friends, the family business was booming, and we were living quite comfortably. Hospital trips had vastly decreased, and overall, I was doing OK health wise and we were all happy. It can only be described as the calm before the storm because God was getting ready to change our lives drastically.

It was in the year of 2000 when my dad started feeling led to move to North Carolina. Why God was calling us to move to North Carolina of all places is beyond me, but I guess that is one reason why I am not God. We soon found out that when the God of the universe tells you to go somewhere and you disobey Him, you are not going to be happy. Dad was miserable, and he tried to stick it out and ignore the call, because his family and friends quite frankly thought he had lost his mind. After a little while my mom could see that it was real and we had to go wherever Dad knew to go, and even though she wasn't looking forward to leaving the life she had and everything she'd ever known, she decided to support her husband and follow wherever God led. Then they had to tell my brother and me we were moving, and you can probably guess we weren't too thrilled. What made me mad was the fact that everything was going to change, and I hated change. However, I was a child and had no clue what the Lord was doing, which is why I had no say in the matter. I got over it soon enough though, and that day eventually came when we packed our lives into tons of boxes and headed down south to the great unknown. We moved on the hope that Dad would soon be singing full time with a bluegrass gospel group, and if that happened Mom did not want to live in the city. Then we got there, and once again everything changed.

Once we finally got there, we began house hunting as a family, but they were not very handicap accessible, and the few that were still were not the right fit. After we explored what seemed like hundreds of homes to two hyperactive kids, Mom and Dad decided that building a house was the best route to go; but as you know, unless you're on "Extreme Makeover: Home Edition", constructing any house takes time. My father strategically picked the city near the local hospital and only an hour from Brenner Children's Hospital to live; that place was Hickory, NC.

However, before we even came down south as a family, my parents came down to visit and since they knew it would take us some time to find or build a house, they rented us a house in Lenoir, NC. So, by the time we got down there, we had a place to live and Dad had a job at a heating and air conditioning company. Then came the process of adapting to a whole new environment, which was not exactly what you would call exciting.

Chapter 10

We officially moved to North Carolina in December of 2002. We settled into our small, cozy house; however, it was not the most ideal home for a handicapped kid. The front door had a very steep hill then a small staircase, while the other two entryways had huge staircases; I might have been roughly eighty pounds then, but that's a lot to have to carry up and down a large flight of stairs. I was trapped in my own home, and that in itself is kind of a downer. On top of that, since we were new to the area my mom decided to home school my brother and I that year: our days usually consisted of sleeping as late as we could get by with, which gradually turned into noon, hopping on the computer to do schoolwork for a few hours, then watching home makeover shows the rest of the day. It was awesome for about a week, then it was boring. I believe that homeschooling can be a wonderful thing if kids are on a schedule and get outside on a regular basis. However, we had no structure that year and considering I could not leave the house often we were cooped up in a tiny five room cubical all day most days. We became stir crazy after about a month or so, and our house hadn't even started getting constructed yet. We had moved down south and soon realized that everyone moved at a snail's pace, which is not that big of a deal under normal circumstances. However, when you're dying to move so you can actually have some room to breathe, it gets a tad annoying when the ones building your house take days off to go fishing and such. After at least a year of waiting, our house was finally completed, and we were ready to move in. In the process of waiting for the house to become livable we really only communicated with our family in Maryland, so when we were all unpacked in our new home it was somewhat hard to become reacquainted with society. In the year 2003 when we were officially settled into our new spacious, accessible home, my parents enrolled my brother and me at public schools. We had never been in the public school system, so that brought on shell shock; and on top of that I was in my first year of middle school while Bubba was in his first year of high school so we couldn't go to the same school where we would at least know one person. If you know me at all you know I could not care less whether or not everyone liked me, but I did want to have at least one close friend. So I started going to Jacobs Fork Middle School in the Fall of '03 and for the first week or two I kept to myself, then I met a girl named Chasity and she quickly became my best friend that year. However, since we did not have any classes that next year in the eighth grade, we went our separate ways. The last year of middle school I was a loner and it was partly because my school was so huge and since I had a speech impediment I couldn't just start talking to someone I hadn't been around at all without them giving me that look like I was speaking some alienated foreign language. After I was finished with junior high, I knew I didn't want to go through the same thing I'd went through that year for four more years, and my brother and I wanted to be in a Christian environment. So, I started my freshmen year of high school along with my brother in his sophomore year of high school at Christian Family Academy.

Chapter 11

The first day of high school at CFA was already looking up since I made some friends fairly quickly. A big reason why I felt so comfortable there was because there were roughly ninety kids in the whole school, along with the fact that most of us believed the same thing. The next four years went by fast in that school and some of my best memories are from there; like the time when me, Bubba, and my cousin Chance concocted one good excuse as to why we were late for school. Let me explain; in the first week of every school year we had spirit week, which is where we dug into The Word, got to know people, and did really fun things to open up the school year. My sophomore year we had spirit week at the elementary campus then came back to the high school campus around 11 AM for classes. On our way back to school one day we decided to take a detour to Bojangles, but then we got lost and didn't get back to school until rather late. Once we finally got there, I had this bright idea that my cousin would unlock my wheels and push me into school while my ventilator was alarming, and my brother was bagging me with an ambu bag. You probably already guessed that they both went for my evil plan and we could have won an Emmy with how scared and worried we acted; that is until the school secretary Mrs. Huffman heard the commotion and ran out to see us with this bewildered look on her face. We busted out laughing right around that time, and even though the whole charade was my idea Bubba and Chance were the ones that got chewed out for it while I just got a stern warning. Then there was that one time when I needed my mom's help with my geometry homework, and she ended up doing it while I sat on my computer playing solitaire.

Although I missed being with my brother my last two years of high school, senior year was great. Of course, that may have been mainly because I had an hour-long study hall with an awesome teacher and my two best friends, so our study hall generally consisted of goofing off while listening to Disney songs... Good times! We also participated in our school Christmas talent show as Alvin and the Chipmunks singing "Christmas Don't Be Late" which was undoubtedly epic beyond all belief. Senior year was also great because no one thought I would live long enough to graduate high school. When graduation finally came, just try to imagine the water works in that church. They were all tears of praise though, praising the King of the universe for being with me through everything. All the close calls, sleepless nights, and medical drama all boiled down to that moment: I did it. We did it, my Savior and me. I may sound crazy, getting all excited over my high school graduation; maybe it was one of those things where you just had to be there to bask in the proof of how gracious my God is. I got that far and intended to live many more years Lord willing because I'd come to the conclusion that God must have some big plans for me, and I was certainly not about to quit and let Him down. My motto in life parallels with the wise words of Charlie Brown: "never ever EVER give up!" I suppose a more adult version of that would be Isaiah 12:2, which says "Behold, God is my salvation; I will trust, and not be afraid: for the LORD JEHOVAH is my strength and my song; He also is become my salvation." True, that is not exactly a motto; but it is a verse I live my life by. On any regular day, I need all the strength I can get.

Chapter 12

Ah, the joys of requiring round-the-clock caregivers...

That is such a nice concept, isn't it? Unfortunately, that idea is sort of like saying "what I love about going to the dentist..." See where I'm going here? There is not much to like about the dentist, aside from the new toothbrush you get on your way out; and that still is not anything to brighten your day unless your hero is the tooth fairy. Dealing with caregivers could be compared to that experience the majority of the time. Let me clarify myself here by saying that I have had many caregivers in the past and still have some today who I've grown very close to and think of as my family; I've still kept in touch with some nurses who worked with me in the past but don't anymore. The challenge for me comes because although I'm more independent than other people in my condition would be, I still have to have a caregiver by my side every minute of every day – whether it's a nurse or private aid. I can be insanely hard on caregivers, but someone has to be. My life is not a matter that I take lightly.

I had one nurse who had been working with me for quite some time, and although we had many differences of opinion, we had never had a serious disagreement – until this one day. While in my sophomore year of high school we were discussing the Terri Schiavo case in my Biology class; in which Terri was hospitalized in 1990 after she collapsed from lack of oxygen to her brain. After months in between the hospital and rehab, Terri Schiavo was slowly regaining her ability to talk when she started saying one-word answers such as "yes" and "no". Fifteen years after Terri Schiavo begun her struggle, after her family fought with the court to take her off of life support, her feeding tube was removed on March 18, 2005 at her husband's request. After 14 days without food or water, Terri Schiavo starved to death. You can say what you want, but I believe with all my heart that that woman still had brain activity and was perfectly fine inside. I also believe that her husband murdered her and should have been charged with murder. She only needed help with breathing and eating on top of not being able to communicate much, and even though I can talk I have the same problems. They had no right to take her life, and since I went to a Christian school, we all believed the same thing, except my nurse. She then decided to put her two cents in and to tell the whole class that Schiavo was not really there mentally and didn't have any brain activity. When my teacher corrected her, she started arguing and pointed out that I am on life support. Already rather frustrated, I asked if she was implying that it would have been right for my parents to kill me and she said yes. That lady had worked with me for two years and that was the last day she worked with me. I am not sure if I will ever be able to completely heal from the hurtful words once uttered so long ago. Every life is precious and worth fighting for, even if they do not fit into this world's twisted view of normal.

I could tell of hundreds of other bad experiences, but this is not a gossip column. Each new conflict I am faced with seems harder than the last; but each new battle teaches me something. Although I do not have nearly enough patience as I should, I have learned that I always need more. I have learned that there is no such thing as a perfect caregiver – they all have their own flaws as I have mine that can sometimes be difficult to overlook. Finding a caregiver that I get along with is like finding a missing piece to the puzzle: sometimes you're given a piece that doesn't quite fit but you have to make it fit because it simply fills the allotted space. This part of my life of relying on caregivers is undoubtedly the hardest part of living with SMA. However, unless God allows scientists to find a cure for Spinal Muscular Atrophy, it is something I will have to live with, but I will go on happy that I am at least here to experience it. God places people in our lives for reasons we may never understand, but the impact we can have on them can be significant; we could be the only trace of Jesus they will ever see. If I have to be a little uncomfortable in order to show my caregivers how amazing my God is so that they can fall in love with Him too, I will gladly do so. What you don't know is that when you find a friend in your caregiver, it is one of the greatest blessings God can give you, and it's in those moments that I am thankful that He put me in the position I'm in to begin with.

Chapter 13

"Few people realize the profound part angelic forces play in human events."

- Billy Graham

Why is it that so many people view angels as scary beings when most have not even encountered such things? That is not how I remember them at all...

I am afraid my angelic encounters may be a tad dull: there were no bright lights, loud noises, or flying acrobatics involved. They looked like any normal person would but wearing white. I mistook them for doctors the first time I saw them; I was laying in my bed during one of the many hospital stays when the chances of me making it through the night were quite slim. I cannot recall the reason for that specific hospital stay, or how old I was at the time. All I remember was how sick I was – the kind of sick where it hurt just to move. I was trying to rest my eyes but seemed restless, so I opened my eyes to see two women in white robes standing beside my bed. They did not speak or even move; they just stood smiling at me. I liked them being there, which was odd because whenever doctors paid me a visit it usually meant I was going to have to do something I didn't want to do, like undergo tests or other unpleasant duties. This was different though. I somehow felt better with them around. I was quite young at the time and in my young tongue I said "Mommy, who are those ladies?" When she asked what ladies, I replied in my confusion "those ladies in the white robes, right there... Don't you see them?" The next time I looked up, they were gone. The next two meetings were when I was 7 years old, right before I got my trach and was in the hospital. What you do not know is that the main reason my doctors and family decided to trach me was because every time I sat up, I stopped breathing. That was a time when everything was touch and go, and they did not know if the next breath would be my last. One night, though, my mom wanted to get me up and in the bath since I had not left my bed in a while. So, they brought me, IV's and all, into the bathroom and put me in the bath; and there they were again, standing there in the doorway. The same two sweet women I met a few hospital visits ago were simply smiling at me, and when I asked who they were, I got the same answer as the last time: there was no one there. Another evening during that same period in A.I. DuPont before I got my trach, my mom sat down to read me a new Barnie book she had bought a few days back. When she got ready to read it, though, I said "you don't have to read that, Mommy. Sister Lindsey read that to me last night." Was it simply the hallucinations of a gravely ill child? Most scientists would think so; but whether or not one believes it, some in this world, for reasons unknown to man, are given the privilege of receiving a small taste of Heaven while being cared for and lulled to sleep by perfect beings best described as angels. I have a spiritual connection that many cannot understand. I recently went under anesthesia to have a procedure done on my hips to reduce pain, and while asleep I had what seemed like a Heavenly experience. I was in a very bright room with Jesus Christ and an angel. I was so happy to be in His presence, and He encouraged me and told me that I was doing a great job and He had much more wonderful things in store for me, so I should go back to life and get back to work. I realize that to some these accounts may seem utterly insane, and that is OK. I know they really happened. Why would the God of the universe choose me to get a small taste of Heaven? I still don't know, but every experience is one that I cherish.

Chapter 14

"Blessed are they that mourn, for they shall be comforted."- Matthew 5:4

I remember it all perfectly still; you would not think it has been so long since everything came crashing down. It was my junior year of high school, and I was stuck by myself since my brother and cousin graduated the year before in 2007. My cousin, Chance, moved down south two years before to live with my grandparents because my family is far from perfect. With a father who's spent well over half of his life in jail and a woman who could not be the mother that he needed, Chance spent the majority of his life with my grandparents until they moved to North Carolina shortly after we moved in 2003. For the next two years we were getting adjusted to our new lives and did not hear much from him, which was not good. We assumed that he had gotten into trouble with his two younger brothers and we were right. So I just hoped and prayed my cousin would come back to us soon; then in the summer of '05 Chance packed up and headed down south to live with my grandparents and attend school with Matt and I at Christian Family Academy. The next four years he went from being my cousin to being a brother, and if you were around us you probably could not tell the difference. We would either ride together to school or meet up with him at the grocery store, and the craziness would continue for the rest of the day. We had so much fun during high school, whether it was goofing off or getting into those occasional adventures. There was that one time when my mom and brother each thought the other one had buckled me into the van and on our way to pick up Chance and his brother who had recently moved here, my wheelchair flipped over. After Bubba quickly examined me and saw I was fine, aside from having a scraped up knee and being tipped over, we had to drive another mile to pick up Chance and his brother Cole so they could help lift me and my three hundred pound chair. Afterwards we were all just laughing about it. We had our fair share of adventures.

After Matt and Chance graduated from CFA in '07, they both went straight to work full time at Dad's business, 72 Degrees of Hickory. However, Bubba was more of management material since he took care of sales and along with that doing the behind-the-scenes work to see that everyone is where they needed to be; and anyone that knew Chance knew that he wasn't a business man. He was an installer, which meant that he went to customers' homes and either installed or repaired heating and air conditioning systems. He was also a goof off: everyone who knew Chance knew he was nothing but a big teddy bear that loved making people laugh. Everything seemed fairly normal from my perspective until the night of December 6, 2007. It was a strange night on that Thursday: I was extremely tired that evening, so I went to bed rather early – around nine o'clock approximately. God gave me the ability to sleep all through the night… He knew I was going to need all my strength to make it through the next day.

I woke up on my own that following morning knowing off the start that something was not right. I had to wake up at 7 AM in order to make it to make it to school by 9, and since I've never been in any way a morning person I would have never woken up that early on my own. I remember lying in bed a few minutes pondering a reason I was staying home from school, and when I could not find one, I called for my nurse. When I asked what time it was and she said ten, I jokingly said "OK, who died?" What I would soon find out would make me promise myself to never ask that question again.

I never did get an answer to my joke of a question, just an awkward laugh from the nurse who then only said my parents would be home shortly. That answer left me waiting, expecting the worst and praying I was overreacting, for maybe the next half hour – it seemed longer, though. When they finally came in my room, all bets were off: this was going to be really bad. They were all there: Mom, Dad, Bubba, and my two grandparents, who had obviously been crying, walked over beside my bed while Mom and Dad sat down beside me. Dad did most of the talking. We got past the small talk and Dad told me the horrible news I had been expecting but not wanting to hear…

"Sis, Chance was on his way home from work last night when he was caught speeding. He tried to outrun the policeman; he went around a turn and became airborne. He crashed into a tree… Chance went home last night." Of course, more was said then that, but that is the gist of what I remember. In those last five words, the realization of it all came crashing down: Chance was not here anymore. He was with his real father, the father that loved him the way his earthly never had. He was with Jesus, away from us. Then the anger came – he had so much more life in him. Why didn't he stop? Why did everyone wait to tell me until the morning after he died? Why did God take my cousin when He could have stopped the collision? Why did everyone's world come unraveling when everything was going so well? I didn't have the answers to such questions then and still don't have them now; all that matters is that during a time when everything around me could have shattered in seconds, the creator of the universe held it all together in His hands. That afternoon – which seemed like a week later – my brother and I went over to my grandparents' house to meet pastors and go through the formalities, and on the way there Bubba played Casting Crown's song "I Know You're There" and the message rang true even more so than before. God was still there just as He had always been, working everything out to make each of us more like Him. What looked like tattered rags to us, God was transforming into a beautiful tapestry that only He can make. We had gotten through many other trials and we were going to get through this by the grace of God.

The next few days were the most exhausting days I had experienced in a long time, if ever. I got so sick of people trying to comfort me with their dumb comments. I am my father's "mini me" in many ways; one being that when faced with major trials I do not enjoy the accompaniment of people and would rather be left alone. So after the funeral when tons of people had thronged to my grandparents' house and were still trying to be comforting, Dad took me home, got us something to eat, and turned on "The Polar Express"; and there was peace.

Chapter 15

After we moved to small town North Carolina and my health began to improve more and more, I was required to have follow-ups with SMA specialists in Winston Salem once a year. I was probably a junior in high school when my mother and I made our hour-long trek to Wake Forest University Medical Center to visit doctors and have a tiring day of medical tests ahead. My entire life my family as well as myself assumed that I had Type 1 SMA, mainly because that was the type my sister had. No one seemed to believe that, though, because people with Type 1 do not live to be much longer than two years – ever. I imagine an exceedingly small percentile of kids with that particular type may live to be ten years of age, but I was 17 at the time and surprisingly very healthy overall. So, when my doctor asked what type of SMA I had and I answered Type 1, she naturally had to have proof to believe it. She sent me to have blood work done, which is always a nightmare since I practically have no veins to work with; but after an hour of poking they got enough blood and sent it off for genetic testing. A week later the results were in – I did indeed have SMA Type 1. Still, nobody could believe it. How could I possibly still be alive and in such great health? The only logical explanation is that for some reason, the God of the universe chose to use me as a vessel to let His glory shine through. My doctor at the time had the excitement of a five-year-old on Christmas morning. The only thing I know to compare it to would be the excitement of a scientist that just discovered a new species. Not only is it alive, but it is healthy too! Now how can we use it? I imagine those words ran through the woman's head during that appointment, but we will never know. She wanted to enroll me in clinical trials, which is a program in which scientists basically treat SMA patients like lab rats: injecting them with the latest concoctions and watching what happens in hopes of finding a cure. At the time it was brought up, though, it did not seem like a bad idea at all. On the contrary, it felt like an answer had finally arrived. No one my age with SMA type 1 had ever been in clinical trials because so few children live to reach adolescence or adulthood. Maybe – just maybe – I was the missing piece to the puzzle that would allow scientists to find a cure. I latched onto that tiny shred of hope and ran with it. Because even though I have always joked about how I don't want to be normal, when I saw the smallest ray of hope that I may be able to walk on this earth, I jumped at it. It was going to take some time to even find out if I could take part in clinical trials, so we left the hospital that day only to return about a month later and find what was or wasn't going to happen in the future. From the moment I was loaded in the van to leave that first doctor's appointment, I did the worst possible thing I could have done: I got my hopes up. I knew full well even then that I should not play the "what if" game, but for some reason my seventeen-year-old mind could not escape the dream world and all the possibilities in it. Life went on as normal for the next few weeks, and upon returning to the hospital I was certain that we were going to hear good news. We got in a room and the doctor came in. She examined me, made sure I was still in good health, and after the formalities approached the topic of clinical trials. Then she dropped the bomb: scientists would not allow me to participate in clinical trials. It seemed like I had a thousand-pound weight on my shoulders. I was ready to fall apart at the seams but couldn't until the doctor left the room, because God knows I cannot cry in front of anyone outside of immediate family. I generally view emotion as a sign of weakness, and I am too stubborn to be seen as weak before anyone but my God. So, I held myself together until she left the room, and right as the door was closing, I lost it. There, in the doctor's office, my mother sat holding me as she has done before, as I cried because I just did not understand. I suddenly felt as if I were in the middle of a Lifetime movie, as I wondered why things could not go my way this time. After all, didn't I deserve it? I composed myself only to remember the question I had just asked I already knew the answer to. I didn't deserve anything. I did not deserve the amazing life God had given me, and I had no right to even question what God was doing. Because in the back of my mind on my worst day I can still hear the gentle voice of my Savior saying "My grace is sufficient", and I suddenly find the strength to not only press on but enjoy my life. Spinal Muscular Atrophy has not overtaken me, nor does it define me, but it has helped mold me into the person I am today, and I do not regret my diagnosis for a minute. I would love to walk one day – and I know I will – even if it is not in this lifetime. Although I have hope that they will find a cure for SMA in my lifetime, however long it takes for me to walk will be worth the wait. Because even through all the bumps along the way, I always know that God knows exactly what He is doing - and that goes for every aspect of life. I, like everyone else, have hopes and dreams for the future, that I have placed at the feet of Jesus. I believe that in His perfect timing, He will give me the desires of my heart. He always has. God does not want to deny us anything; He just wants us to trust Him completely. That is not to say, though, that He is some magic genie who only exists to grant your every wish – the way of the cross is so much deeper than that. God's ways and man's ways are polar opposites: one viewpoint claims that whatever you want you find a way to get it and you'll be happy, while the other claims that you should ultimately ask God what He wants for our lives and follow Him and find true happiness. God is a father who wants the absolutely best for us, and all He asks is that we have patience. Patience is even required to reach Heaven - the greatest of blessings. Trust in His plan. In the end, He promises it will all be worth the wait.

Chapter 16

We all have a best friend: someone you can tell anything to, and they do not judge you. Someone who you love being around, who you stay up late with talking to, act goofy around: someone who loves you just for being you. My best friend's name is Jesus Christ. I want to be just like Him. When most of my other so-called best friends have abandoned me, He is always stuck around. It is safe to say that I always stand out in a crowd – many have not come across an individual quite like me before, what with the trach and vent and all. I have come to the realization that there is a certain stigmatism that comes along with being handicapped. People automatically think that I am mentally handicapped and do not even attempt to get to know me to see who I really am. But I am not simply different on the outside, you see; for there has been a supernatural change inside of me. I did not notice how different I was from the rest, though, until I became an outsider.

I had gone through periods of being an outcast ever since age 13. 7th grade went better than 8th. Afterwards I tried so hard to make friends, but ultimately it just did not happen. I was the new kid in town, and as if middle school is not hard enough anyway, kids are not very welcoming to kids they have not known their entire lives. Not only that, but have you seen me? Many have never seen someone quite like me and it can be scary. No one was ever mean to me through junior high, but no one went out of their way to be a friend to me with the exception of one for a brief period of time. I soon found a safe haven in my local church – but even that didn't last long.

When I turned fifteen everyone my age at church was changing except for me. Kids my age were going different directions and trying different things, and I was fine where I was. My version of fun was playing Webkinz computer games and baking cookies, seriously. I wanted more than anything just to have one real friend, but I had been betrayed and rejected more times than I could count. I was utterly invisible. After my brother and now sister-in-law graduated out of youth group, I would sit in the corner completely alone every Wednesday night without anyone stopping to even notice my existence. My family saw it; the church leaders saw it; but no one knew how to change it. What is worse is having people that talk to you online but ignore you in public. I did not understand; what had I done to be treated so badly by people who were supposed to be my brothers and sisters in Christ? Maybe I was not fun enough or cool enough; or maybe people are too close minded to accept that which they do not understand. I did not change per se, but after enduring this treatment for over a year, I had grown more worn and bitter than I had ever been before. I decided I had to leave, and we all left the church together. We spent the next four years church hopping, searching for a place to belong. We visited places together and separately. Even while searching, though, I had bad experiences with churches. I found one church that, even though it was completely untraditional and different than any other church I had been to, had sweet people that made me feel like perhaps I could call that place my new "home". Alas, it was all just too good to be true. I did not agree with how the church leadership was conforming to the world so others would think their church was cooler than anyone else's. Unfortunately, they did not really care what I had to say, and I ultimately left there disappointed yet again.

I honestly do not know if I will ever completely heal from the wounds that church people have left on my heart throughout the years. I do know that I no longer have any ill feeling towards any church; I simply think that too many times people change the church instead of letting God change them. I can now look back on that particular time in my life and say it was one of the best things that has happened to me, because through that I learned that religion and Christianity are two very different lifestyles. I learned that many times lost people are more loving than those who sit on the front pews of church every week. In the end I realized that it does not matter what everyone else in the church does, because all that matters is my relationship with God. Whether or not my fellow churchgoers like me is irrelevant. Maybe it is not always a bad thing to be invisible, as long as people can see Christ rather than me. Theodore Roosevelt made a profound statement when he said "I care not what others think of what I do, but I care very much about what I think of what I do. That is character."

Chapter 17

Life is constantly changing and at times quite scary, but always rewarding when you make it to where you know God wants you to be… But how do you know where God wants you to be? We know that His plans aren't always the same as our plans and His thoughts aren't always our thoughts, but I want my thoughts and plans and everything about me to be so much like him that people know I am a child of the Most High King. Unfortunately, I am an over thinker who, for many years, was paranoid of making a mistake in terms of a career path and letting my Heavenly Father down. For a long time I was under the impression the will of God was one particular dot on the map of life, and that if I didn't somehow land on that same dot, I was a failure in God's eyes. It was not for years later that I concluded that God probably is not as strict as I envisioned Him being. After graduating high school, I enrolled in community college and began getting my Associate's in Arts because that looks good on a resume, but I had no idea what to do with my life. And if you're really asking yourself the question, I think you are, yes, I actually wanted to and made plans to have a career. I wanted to earn my own money, and productively use whatever ability God gave me. But do I even have any abilities?

I am a computer dork who spends at least 90% of my time messing around on my laptop, trying to figure out techie tricks that others don't know about while reading as little instructions as humanly possible. Again, I know what you are thinking: how can someone who cannot lift her own hand operate a computer? Technology is a beautiful thing. Around the age of 12, I met with a team of assistive technology experts to come up with a new way for me to work my computer since I was losing what little amount of strength I had and could no longer use the Trackball mouse. We tried a few different assistive technology programs, including speech recognition, which usually ended in failure. Eventually, though, I found the perfect software: one that would allow me to operate an entire computer with simple synchronized clicks of one tiny button. I have used it ever since. It is how I socialize online, how did done schoolwork for years, and how I wrote the majority of this book. I could go into so much more depth on everything I can do through my computer, but I will spare you the details.

I knew I at least had one ability but did not know how to use it. I wanted to help people, so career paths like graphics design and website builder were out. I love studying psychology and am kind of obsessed with Criminology. I guarantee I have seen every Criminal Minds re-run ever played on A&E (don't judge me). How could I work in computers, help others, and maybe incorporate some sort of detective work? I finally came across the perfect college major: Cyber Crime Technology. My college offered a two-year degree in this, which is basically another terminology for Computer Forensics. If you are still lost – like most are when I am attempting to explain the profession I am aiming for – I want to be an investigative geek like the ones you see on television crime dramas. I also like the thoughts of being a behavioral analyst.

I began classes to attain a degree in Cyber Crime Technology and absolutely loved most of it. What a wonderful feeling it is to believe that you are on the track God wants you to be on, even if it took a little longer than I would have liked to get there. I want to use my God-given abilities to help people, and the criminal justice field gave me an outlet to do that. After five years and a multitude of health-related setbacks, I was finally able to graduate with two different associate degrees: one in Art and another in Cyber Crime Technology. It was a big deal. My family and I had relocated back to the state of Maryland that previous year in 2014, but we made a special trip back down south so I could roll across that stage and accept my diplomas.

In August of 2015, I began attending the University of Maryland online, dual majoring in Cybersecurity and Criminal Justice. I graduated from the University of Maryland – University College in December of 2018 with a dual major bachelor's degree in Criminal Justice and Cybersecurity, and plan on pursuing a Master's in Forensic Psychology.

Today, in 2020, I utilize eye gaze technology to operate my Microsoft Surface Pro tablet.

I have no idea what career God will give me when I am finished with all my schooling, but if I can help people, I'll be happy. My dream job would be with the FBI, but who knows what God has in store? I am not about to limit Him in any way – He knows what He is doing.

Chapter 18

"Consider it pure joy, my brothers, when you face trials of many kinds, for you know that the testing of your faith develops perseverance."-James 1:2-3

One of the side effects that my disease had on my body is that my mouth did not grow normal. When my upper jaw grew in, it somehow protruded out further than it should have and was further up: sort of jammed into my skull. My lower jaw, on other hand, was sunk back much further than it should have been. The result of these two deformities left me unable to close my mouth whatsoever and thus unable to be clearly understood. That made social interaction with strangers quite difficult because whoever was taking care of me ended up also being my translator. It took a few days of being around me for someone to understand my speech. This particular handicap was always rather frustrating to me and became even more so as I got older. The fact that some people just try to placate me by smiling and nodding rather than asking me to repeat myself makes it even worse. Whenever I know that whoever I am talking to didn't understand what I said, I will ask if they caught what I had said. When they reply yes, I then will say "OK, so what did I just say?" It is quite entertaining watching their faces as they try to come up with the correct answer. What people fail to understand is that in doing things such as that in hopes of making me feel comfortable, you make me feel stupid and inadequate. People try so hard not to offend anyone, but all I want is for you to be real with me. Nonetheless, I always hated the challenges that not being able to close my mouth presented me with. I was unable to interact with others like I would like to; I always had little ones coming up to me asking "why does her mouth look like that?" I wanted so badly to be like everyone else in that one aspect, but every doctor I asked said it could not be done. I had braces all through high school, and while that definitely helped looks wise, I still wasn't able to close my mouth and my orthodontist assured me that I most likely would never be able to. It is hard to accept that something won't happen when you want it so bad, but that is just what I did. I still always held onto a small bit of hope, though, that God would make a way for it to be in His perfect timing. The only problem was that I have difficulty being patient at times. I wonder if God ever looks down on us, laughing, saying "my child, I have so many amazing plans for you! Just wait a little while longer."

It was at some point during the year 2011 that my dentist discovered I had a few very painful cavities that needed to be filled, and unfortunately my mouth is too small to allow dentists to do any kind of dental work with me awake. So, my dentist referred me to a well renowned oral surgeon in Charlotte, NC location of the Carolina Medical Center who would conduct the surgery. At my consultation, my mother brought up the question we had asked every other doctor: is there any way you can help her close her mouth? And he said yes. Granted, he also said that it would be a long process and it certainly wouldn't be easy; but he said that if I wanted to be able to close my mouth, he could make it happen. I jumped at the opportunity, and so the journey began. I had to get braces for the second time in my life in order to align both top and bottom teeth so they would meet when my mouth closed post-op. I had to have molds made of my mouth and the surgical team made a three dimensional replica of my skull to serve as a guide. I had CAT scans done and had my own team of medical experts that took intricate measurements of my mouth. They had a game plan that they went over multiple times with what order they would make cuts. Extra bags of blood platelets were brought in just in case I lost blood too rapidly. This was a very major surgery and so the surgeons took all possible precautions they could. There was a strange sense of excitement in the air because no doctor or patient had ever endeavored down this path with having this kind of disability. The day finally came for surgery and we were all ready for it to be over with. In spite of all the preparation we had done up until that point, I still hadn't taken into account the amount of pain that I was in for. My doctor had warned me that I would certainly have some pain and numbness, but he did not seem to think that it would be that bad, and that put me at ease. My mother is a wise woman and kept trying to explain to me that as serious as this surgery was going to be, I was undoubtedly going to be in an enormous amount of pain. I was too excited to listen. This was something I had always wanted, and because it was within my grasp, I made the naïve mistake of thinking that it would somehow come easily. I had never been more wrong.

They wheeled me back into the operating room at Charlotte Carolina Medical Center at 7 AM on January 29, 2013. I wasn't terrified at all until I was actually in the OR watching my surgeons gather around a desk and go over the game plan one last time. There was no room for error; one wrong cut could end my life. These surgeons were the best in the nation, but they were still only men and men can make mistakes. As I began to drift out of consciousness, I asked God to guide their hands and use me in this situation to bring honor to His name. And then the darkness came.

A little over six hours later, the process was successfully complete. I awoke in Recovery crying from the pain. I was soon transferred to a room in the ICU where I remained for the next three days. I had some amazing nurses and respiratory therapists who took great care of me and made me feel special on my birthday in spite of being where I was. I could not rest at all in the hospital due to the excruciating pain, nausea, and the fact that nurses had to check my vitals every 1-2 hours. Our first night there was horrible, and by the end of it, Mom was in my bed holding me as I cried myself to sleep. The next day and night wasn't much better because the nurses still wouldn't let me rest since they were constantly giving medication, checking my vitals, and sending me downstairs to get more CAT scans done to ensure that my bones were aligned properly. That night, Mom and I woke up in the early morning to find a big banner reading "Happy Birthday Amber" that my nurses had made me and hung up in my room. It is in moments like that that I am thankful for God blessing me with sweet people who take care of me. The following day, February 1st, my Mom, Dad, and brother decided it was time to take me home because I was unable to get the proper rest I so desperately needed. My doctor released me, and my three family members very carefully escorted me out to Dad's truck where I laid for the hour-long trip home. I would love to tell you that the recovery process from that point on was a cake walk, but I would be lying. I had never been in so much pain before in my life. I was prescribed the highest dose of pain medicine, and they were as effective as popping Tic-Tac's in terms of masking the pain. They did, however, prove effective in making me constantly drowsy and irritable. I did not want to talk to anyone or do anything – I would not even get out of bed. I did not want to eat. I could not move without crying from the pain. I could not sleep because of the narcotics. I had facial paralysis, but still felt pain and had frequent nerve spasms through my jaws. I had no idea how long it would take me to heal, or how I would make it that long. I remember sitting in my doctor's office sobbing – something I never do – asking him to help me get relief, and he couldn't. I spent the first week after coming home in bed doing absolutely nothing, and my health was deteriorating because of it. I remember one day my mom came down and gave me a reality check, and although I was angry at what she said, it made me stop and examine my heart. It was then that I realized many things: God had not forsaken me, there was a reason for all of this even though I didn't know what that reason was, and it was time to stop sulking and fight. That day I made the decision to cut down my pain medicine dosage by over half. I got out of bed and started eating by mouth. It was still Winter outside and though I could not go outside, my family would load me in the van, and go driving around just to get out. I could not taste or smell anything since my surgery, but I and my nurses would make recipes for my family or bake cookies. Did this make everything perfect? Certainly not. I still had bad days and, though I refused to take medicine, I believe I went through a short bout of depression due to the overwhelming amount of pain that I was dealing with daily. Even though I could not see it then, each day I was growing a little stronger. I sat down one day and wrote out two lists side by side: one with everything I was suffering from, and another with all the blessings that God has given me. The blessings outweighed the struggles by far. At the very bottom of the list, typed in bold and highlighted for emphasis, I scribed four simple words: Everything will be alright. And it was. One month, two months… Six months down, and although I still had a bit of swelling, the pain was finally gone. Somewhere towards the end of my healing process, I had two custom designed one-of-a-kind hooks manufactured, and drilled into one side of my and lower jaws. This unique invention has allowed me to place a small elastic band on the hooks, which closes my mouth and acts as a muscle. I am now able to swallow easier than before. I also speak much clearer now, but still need a little help with translating at times – and that's alright. I have found much more confidence in communicating with others, and for that I am eternally grateful. To God be the glory! He is faithful.

Chapter 19

One of my favorite passages of scripture can be found in John 9:1-3:

Now as Jesus passed by, He saw a man who was blind from birth. And His disciples asked Him, saying, "Rabbi, who sinned, this man or his parents, that he was born blind?" Jesus answered, "Neither this man nor his parents sinned, but that the works of God should be revealed in him."

"Why do bad things happen to good people?"

This question plagues people worldwide, regardless of religious affiliation, race, age, or region. Why would a God of love let His children suffer? Does He even care? Is He listening to my prayers? There are just some things in this life that we will never be able to understand until we reach Heaven, and that is OK. However, there are some things of which I am sure of:

God does care. He loves you more than you can fathom.

He hears every single prayer you say aloud and those you store inside your heart.

He answers every prayer, regardless of whether it is the answer you want.

He is unpredictable, but His plans are perfect, and He is good.

Let's really examine this question of "Why do bad things happen to good people?" First, define good. What constitutes as a good person? Because according to scripture, none of us are good in comparison to the God of the universe. In fact, according to Isaiah 64, all of our righteous acts are like filthy rags. Do you know what "filthy rags" translates to? The term originates from the Hebrew root 'ed for filthy and refers to results of a woman's menstrual cycle. Disgusting, right? The point I am trying to make is that none of us are good to begin with, and so the question in essence is invalid. We are worthless, and yet God lovingly bestows grace on us time and time again. Also, if Jesus Christ, who was a perfect image of God made in flesh, had to face suffering Himself, what makes you think that you deserve better than Him?

See, as many already know, God's original manuscript for mankind was a perfect utopia in which evil could not enter. The original version of man and woman, Adam and Eve, were created by God Himself to rule over the Garden of Eden, and they were given one commandment and dominion over everything else. Unfortunately, they chose to sin against God and blew their shot at a perfect and carefree life in face-to-face fellowship with God. That one act of eating from the forbidden tree brought sin into the world forevermore. It was not God's fault in the least that mankind betrayed Him in going against His will and thus tarnishing the original concept of a perfect sin-free world, and once it was done it was done it couldn't be undone.

The story of the origin of sin still does not help you cope when you are in the middle of a storm, though. When your child has just been diagnosed with Leukemia, you do not want to hear Bible stories or philosophies on why this tragedy is happening. Life is not always logical, and we as humans are not able to see the bigger picture because we are not God. We are too blind to realize that every trial that comes into our lives is simply a new opportunity for us to strengthen our faith and encourage others. I heard a quote once that went something like this: life is 10% of what happens to me and 90% of how I react to it.

I will never know why bad things happen to good people, but I believe that if I wasted precious time searching for the answer, I would miss out on some great blessings God has given me. Life is so much better when I accept the inevitable, give God all my heartache, and enjoy life to the fullest. I have a horrible disease, but I love my life because of the joy I have. People that go through hell on earth and come out victoriously are the ones who have unshakable faith. When coal is forced through levels of extremely high heat, diamonds are formed. You are a diamond, darling – now is your time to shine.

Chapter 20

Despite the obvious setbacks that my physical disability presents on a daily basis, I have always loved helping people. When I was eight years old, my father and I worked out an arrangement where I would receive a dollar for every "A" I got on tests in school. Halfway through the semester, I had a plan that I had not told anyone about yet. I had accrued a small fortune of about $45 by the time Christmas rolled around and I unveiled my secret: I wanted to give Christmas gifts to a less fortunate family who needed help that year with the measly amount of cash I had earned from my good grades. My brother, being his entrepreneurial self, suggested I invest some of the money for the future, but I just could not do it. Of course, my parents chipped in at that point, and we were able to give Christmas to a single mother and her two children. What an amazing experience it was! From that point on, the desire grew in my heart to help people and share the love of God with those who are hurting.

I have always loved kids – even when I was a kid myself. Kids are nonjudgmental; they are not afraid of those who are different, although they are curious. Kids are always ready to hear about the love of Jesus. Kids are innocent and open to anything. They are awesome without trying. These are the reasons why, as I grew older, I wanted to minister specifically to children. I was under the impression that God was leading me to give the gospel to hospitalized children, but throughout the years He has redirected me to be on His perfect path time and time again.

Our first year of doing Candy Cane Kids was successful, though it did not seem like it would be until the very end. I had contacted a local children's hospital and explained my mission and asked if I could come deliver wrapped gifts that had multiple toys and a Bible in them and distribute them to the children. We worked out an arrangement and set up a date and time for me to bring everything. I gathered the funds that I family and I had raised and bought a multitude of toys, books, teddy bears, and Bibles. I also bought about 200 large gift bags and filled them to the top with goodies. I then labeled the bags with the appropriate ages and genders that were to receive them, to make the distribution process easier. The day before I was scheduled to deliver everything, I called the hospital once again to confirm that I could come. Apparently, they had changed their minds when they realized that I was sharing the gospel of Jesus Christ along with the gifts, and informed me that I was not welcome to bring my presents to their establishment for political reasons. So there I was, about five days before Christmas, with 200 wrapped gifts in my home and nowhere to take them. I was defeated to say the least. I had come so far – why was this happening now? Thankfully, my family is amazing and did everything within their power to see that I had a place with needy children for me to give to. And so, we did. We ended up donating all of the gifts to children in social services. Whether they were foster children or abused, the recipients of these gifts needed some hope. It was from there that I came up with the name Candy Cane Kids and our official slogan "Bringing Hope to the Hopeless". From that point on, the mission of Candy Cane Kids has flourished and still continues to do so. Not only did I introduce letters that accompany each gift that are from me personally, that tell each child how much Jesus loves them and how they can ask Him into their hearts and have hope; the following year I began giving out Bibles along with every gift too. Of course, this in turn made it even harder for any medical establishment to allow us to give to sick or handicapped children; but I have stood my ground on this subject. Organizations have told me that they will accept the gifts if I omit the Bibles, but the entire goal of this ministry is to share the gospel of Jesus Christ with children, and without that our work is in vein. In turn, God has richly blessed me for my obedience, and is constantly opening up new doors for Candy Cane Kids. Over the past ten years, Candy Cane Kids Ministry has given Christmas to well over 3000 needy children. Overall, we have ministered to kids in the Department of Social Services, orphanages, a battered family shelter, a Crisis Pregnancy Center, and underprivileged children living in trailer parks and Section 8 Housing Complexes throughout our local community. In 2015 I partnered with my home church and also with retired professional football player Ray Sydnor, and together we were able to minister to hundreds of children throughout the entire state of Maryland. My heart's desire is still to minister to sick or terminally ill, and I believe that God will allow that dream to come true in His perfect timing. Even if He does not, though, He is still good.

Orchestrating the latest projects for Candy Cane Kids every year is not easy, but always worth all the work put into it. My mother is my right-hand lady who helps me with all physical aspects of this charity, and everyone who I enlist to help me put everything together understands that I'm the head person behind the scenes that just needs some man power to help me get things done. I always tell my family "I'm the brains and you're the muscles". I have met so many people who enjoy helping share the gospel through this ministry year after year. The mere assembly of this ministry is something that only God could do, and so I plan on continuing to fulfill the mission of Candy Cane Kids until or unless God tells me to stop. Like every other area of my life, I have given God the wheel to direct me wherever He chooses because He knows what is best. This is His show; I am just the organizer.

Chapter 21

Our current generation is facing an epidemic of massive proportions, that is robbing people of their joy and drive to live: the plague of the self-pitying person. You may laugh at the thought, but you know it is true. Everyone is susceptible to falling into self-pitying mindsets; I believe it is one of Satan's most valuable tools of destruction. If he can infiltrate your mind, he can destroy your life. People do not realize the seriousness of even having one negative thought, but one becomes two and two becomes ten, and before long your life is practically ruined, and nothing satisfies you. And what kind of outcome does that bring about? One of a miserable soul living a miserable life, and nothing more. Somewhere along the way, people forgot what we were designed for. The ultimate goal of human life is not to merely survive day after day, drearily waiting for death to come. We were made to thrive and enjoy the great blessing of life that God has bestowed upon each of us. If we allow ourselves to embrace the joy that can truly only come through Christ, we unleash within ourselves a power that can transform our lives and give us true happiness even in the trials of life. Everyone goes through hard times, and now and then we all fall down... What defines us is how well we rise after falling.

I have never been one to complain and become irritated when I am around people who are negative. I believe life is what you make it. If you hate your life, change it. If you do not like your job, get a new one – even if that means going back to school. If your home life is terrible, fight with all you have to make it a happy home. God gave you the ability to decide the theme of your life; why not make it a good one? Your life could always be worse, so be thankful for the blessings you do have. Not only is self-pitying unnecessary and unattractive, but it is also dangerous. Oswald Chambers once wrote "Beware of allowing self-consciousness to continue because by slow degrees it will awaken self-pity, and self-pity is Satanic." Satanic, you say? I believe so. There is great power in the mind. Life is hard; if it wasn't, we would have no reason to long for Heaven. If we simply give up on life when we come to the first bump in the road, though, we miss out on reaping the greatest of blessings that can only be found in the midst of a storm.

I am nowhere near perfect – I never claimed to be, but I am a genuinely happy and positive person because of the overflowing joy and peace God has given me. I know that my situation could always be worse, and I am grateful for the many blessings I do have. I cannot walk, but I can roll around in the coolest electrical wheelchair you'll ever see – and walking seems vastly overrated, anyway. I cannot breathe on my own, but I have a compact ventilator that goes everywhere with me and does not stop me from doing anything. I cannot move, but I have done more in 29 years than most people do in 100. Life is hard, but God is good. 1 Peter 1:6-8 says "In this you greatly rejoice, though now for a little while you may have had to suffer grief in all kinds of trials. These have come so that your faith—of greater worth than gold, which perishes even though refined by fire—may be proved genuine and may result in praise, glory and honor when Jesus Christ is revealed. Though you have not seen him, you love him; and even though you do not see him now, you believe in him and are filled with an inexpressible and glorious joy". Likewise, there is much beauty that can be found in going through difficult times. Take a pearl, for example. A pearl is beautiful and perfect, but have you ever thought about what it had to go through to get that way? It begins when a foreign object – usually a grain of sand - somehow enters into the inner bed of an oyster and gets lodged in there, unable to escape, which causes a great deal of pain for the oyster. To protect itself and ease its discomfort, the oyster then secretes several layers of a smooth, hard crystalline called nacre substance around the irritant. Once the source of pain is completely encased in the milky white calcium carbonate substance, you have a glorious little pearl. This type of metamorphosis is not just with pearls: we see it again with diamonds that are formed far beneath the earth's surface when carbon is subjected to extremely high amounts of heat and pressure. Does that sound enjoyable to you? Or when a caterpillar becomes encased in a tight, restrictive cocoon with barely enough room to breathe before it transforms into a majestic butterfly or moth? That does not seem very fun to me. Beautiful things do not just happen without something or someone going through something unpleasant. The best of things never come easy, and nothing easy is worth doing. God wants only the best for us, if we are strong and patient enough to wait for our beautiful metamorphosis.

I constantly strive to be positive, and from the outside it might look as though I have it all together, but rest assured I do not. I am not perfect, and neither are you, and if you think that's what being a Christian is about, then I pray He saves you and shows you the truth. I have my days where nothing goes right and life in general is too much to bear. There are times when I am overwhelmed and break down, and that is alright. Christ, in His time on earth, promised a hard life with a lot of sorrow for all who chose to follow Him, but He also promised to give us strength to make it through the difficult days. It is not a sin to cry, though it took me quite a while to realize. You can have an occasional meltdown, as long as you don't stay there too long. God is not finished with you yet, and when you're on the other side of the mountain you will be stronger and better for it. You are allowed to fall sometimes, but never forget to get back up and keep fighting. In the end, it will all be worth it – I promise.

Chapter 22

I have to laugh at the thought of anyone believing that the road that leads to Jesus isn't an easy one to walk. Filled with spiritual potholes and roadblocks, it is not always pleasant. As I have stated before, it most definitely is worth it, to have the God of the universe by your side guiding you through this life. He makes everything beautiful and brings true joy to those who seek Him wholeheartedly. But at the same time, Job was not lying when he said, "Man that is born of a woman is of few days and full of trouble." Christians are not called to live a comfortable life free of trouble. Christians are called to follow Christ, no matter the cost. Francis Chan said it best in his book Crazy Love: Overwhelmed by a Relentless God: "God doesn't call us to be comfortable. He calls us to trust Him so completely that we are unafraid to put ourselves in situations where we will be in trouble if He doesn't come through."

It was in the year 2013 when this particular chapter of my story began. We had been living in North Carolina for eleven years when we started discussing the possibility of relocating back to Maryland – where our family originated. For myself, it was not the most logical thing to want to move back. After all, I had just moved into my custom-designed apartment just one year before. I had an amazing group of nurses and aids who loved me as their own and would drive me wherever I wanted to go and do whatever I wanted to do. I had my own van and complete freedom to come and go as I pleased. My family and I were just as close as we had ever been. I was attending classes on campus and online. Candy Cane Kids was flourishing – in a different direction than I originally planned, but nonetheless it was. From the outside looking in, my life was as close to perfect as it could get. Yet on the inside, I was not happy. Since graduating high school in 2009, I did not have any close friends, and although my immediate family was always there for me, I longed for a sense of fellowship. I tried getting involved with a Christian club at my college hoping to make connections there, only to have my e-mails ignored. I tried desperately to find a church whose parishioners would love me as their own, but if you recall, I described that endeavor a few chapters back and as much as I tried it just never worked out. Once my family and I settled on a church where we agreed on the preaching, I mainly kept to myself and tried to stay out of everyone's way because if I left my walls up I wouldn't get hurt again. The problem with this philosophy is that as hard as some try to not get attached to others, we were all created by God with an innate desire to feel a sense of community – and I didn't really have that. I had felt like an outsider on and off since moving to North Carolina in 2002, but I felt like one now more than ever. Nobody was ever ugly to me, but very rarely did anyone ever go out of their way to show me kindness. Lots of people knew me, but nobody ever contacted me just to catch up. My difficulty making meaningful relationships in school and church had brought me to a place of bitterness that no child of God should come to. I didn't care. While my family was still my rock, and I was furthering my education, and my love for the Lord was not shaken, nothing else mattered to me. I gave up trying to make friends because there was no use in it. A large portion of my father's family still resided in the state of Maryland, and I began to grow homesick for the north. I knew it was a lost cause because my family surely wouldn't consider making such a life changing move – again – just because I was struggling. Nevertheless, I believed God was wanting me to share my heart with my family, and so I did. What I soon discovered was that God was already aligning all of our hearts toward the same direction. One year later, the family business sold, then our home, then my brother's family's home, and twelve years after we first began that chapter of our lives, we repacked all we knew into boxes and headed back home where our story began. The only difference was we left as a family of four and returned with two more precious people. It was all scary and exciting and I had absolutely no idea what was in store. The truth was that as happy as my heart was to be back home, closer to family and friends, I was about to enter a whole new realm of uncomfortableness that I was unprepared for.

We moved back to Cecil County, Maryland, in August of 2014. My father, brother, and mother immediately bought and took over the family HVAC company that my uncle started several years before. Taking over a new company is no easy task and making it into the most successful business it can be is even harder. But my family has never backed down from a challenge – we merely embrace them. However, add to the challenge one more: I had yet to be approved for nursing in the state of Maryland. The approval process was a long and tedious one, and the lady who made the call if I could have nursing was anything but helpful. For the first month of settling in, I had no nursing services whatsoever. It was up to my family and the first part-time aid we hired to care for me that first month until I got approved for nursing and got connected to a private duty nursing agency. Then another problem arose: the area we live in is so close to Delaware that nurses can easily go work there and in turn make more money there than in

Maryland. This, unfortunately, left me with the less-than-best nurses, like an elderly dear who couldn't hear my ventilator alarms, and the one who pulled my trach out and panicked, leaving me without a trach for about thirty minutes, all while screaming "are you going to die?" at me. But I did not die. After a few moments of shear panic I realized I was beginning to feel lightheaded, and so I had a little talk with Jesus and made up my mind that if He had gotten me this far, he could handle this. My breathing slowed as I patiently awaited my mother to come to my rescue. She was flying down the interstate to get home to me when the Lord spoke to her and told her that my trach had come out. She then telephoned the hysterical nurse and told her to put the trach back in. That nurse did not return. That was one of the worst experiences, but there were many more that followed within the next year. I knew it would not be easy to find a great team of nurses like the ones I had in North Carolina, but I figured after six months we would have had a few keepers. It seemed, in this aspect of life, we would take one step forward and three steps back. Agencies were unable to staff my case, so we posted ads on social media. We found what seemed to be the perfect fit: a registered nurse who had previously worked in the military. We hired her to be my full-time day shift nurse. She didn't mind driving me around like my North Carolina nurses had – things were looking up. Then a few weeks into the job she suddenly changed. Her bubbly disposition disappeared and was replaced by a snippy attitude. She would fall asleep when she should have been taking care of me. She told us she was pregnant, but she would secretly sneak outside multiple times per shift to grab a smoke. She was nicer when we were out in public, so I tried to go out more often. Then one day she took me to the nail salon and right when we entered the salon said she would be right back. Nurses should never leave their patients unattended, but I was well past the point of frustration and assumed she went for a smoke. I had not taken into account the fact that she took my wallet with her. She came back inside after a few minutes and was incredibly nice the remainder of the day. The following day she claimed she was having a miscarriage and had to go home. My mom came home to relieve her, and it was then that I did a routine bank account check and discovered $40 had been withdrawn from an ATM located just outside the nail salon we had been at the previous day. Apparently, she remembered my PIN from a past grocery shopping trip. My mother confronted her via text, and she confessed. Authorities were consulted, charges were filed, and eventually we went to court, where we learned that she was indeed still pregnant and was also a drug addict. With one mistake, the woman lost her family, job, and most likely her nursing license. But there's more: because of her mistake, nurses from that point on refused to drive me anywhere out of fear that they would lose their license. That presented a whole new dilemma, as I felt like a prisoner in my own home. It was during that time that I also came to the realization that ultimately the state of Maryland did not care about me and my quality of life. I am merely a number to them. I do not like rules and do not take kindly to people – especially those from the government – telling me what I can and cannot do, but you can't always get what you want. We would have to work out a different arrangement where I could have a personal driver or God would have to change the hearts of my future nurses so they would be comfortable with transporting me. It was going to be a long, difficult process, but eventually God would bring about a wonderful team of caregivers… I just had to be patient… Right?

Life in Maryland has not been quite what I thought it would be. Who knows? I might end up back in North Carolina one day. Only God knows what the future holds. The grass isn't always greener on the other side, but God is unchanging and can use any situation to bring Glory to Himself and His ultimate plan if we put our lives in His hands. Paul testified to the Philippians, saying "for I have learned to be content whatever the circumstances." We as Christians need to learn to be content in any situation – even the most uncomfortable ones. In the midst a difficult circumstance, it is important to remember that it will not last forever. We are but clay, and it takes time for The Potter to mold us to be more like Him.

Chapter 23

Despite the troubles I had with caregivers and the healthcare system since moving back, great things were happening. It was decided that I would be seen at John Hopkins Medical Center for all of my medical needs, being as it's one of the top hospitals in the nation and it's a mere 45 minute drive from our home. The first visit I made was to see Dr. Thomas Crawford; a well-known neurologist and one of the best doctors that specializes in SMA. My mother and father had not been to John Hopkins since the death of my sister 26 years prior, so it was emotional for Mom being back. We checked me in and waited for me to be called back to be seen. We were talking when Dr. Crawford himself came out to the waiting room and introduced himself to me. Then something crazy happened: he asked me if I remembered him. I answered no and he replied that he knew my sister. When Lindsey was in the hospital for so many months battling for her life, Dr. Crawford was just beginning his medical career as a doctor. He worked in the lab and was not allowed to work one-on-one with patients just yet, but he had heard that there was a baby staying in the Pediatric ICU with SMA and he couldn't help himself. He would sneak in to visit her when nobody was around. She was the first SMA baby he had ever encountered firsthand. That information alone was overwhelming, then he took us back to the exam room. He left the room for a brief time and came back with a large folder with the name "Lindsey Amber Stewart" written across the front of it. It was my sister's medical files. As my mother was flipping through the pages detailing her baby's short life, the doctor thanked her and my father for allowing them to allow them to conduct an autopsy on Lindsey, explaining that he and other doctors still study her autopsy slides today as they continue to search for a cure for SMA. He then mentioned that they were closer than they had ever been before. Of course, that was good for Mom to hear, and I somehow felt even more connected to my sister than I had before. He then went back to business and began my examination, at the end of which concluding that I was one of the oldest SMA patients he had ever seen and by far the most functioning one. He was quite impressed with how far I had come in life, yet silently scoffed when I attributed such success to Christ alone. That is alright, though - I know the truth even if no one else believes it. In one day, it seemed like our family had come full circle. It truly seemed like God had brought us back to Maryland for a divine purpose. Who knows; maybe we came back because a cure really was coming soon, and I had to be here to get it? Or maybe not, and that's OK. God is constantly surprising me in how He is orchestrating my life and I do not want to make the mistake of limiting Him in any way. We do not always understand why certain things happen in life, and it certainly isn't our right to know it all. But when God graciously pulls back the curtain the slightest bit to give us a glimpse of the beautiful masterpiece that He is making out of our messed up lives, it puts everything in perspective and reveals the power of a gracious, loving God. He really is in control, and everything we go through in this life is for a greater good that will be revealed to us one day in Glory.

On December 23, 2016, The U.S. Food and Drug Administration approved Spinraza (also known as Nusinersen) - the first drug approved to treat patients with Spinal Muscular Atrophy. This was huge. What a miracle this was! Babies can be saved from the near promise of death. This drug, which is administered via injection into the patient's spinal column multiple times in the first year of treatment then once a year from thereon out, has shown incredible results when given to SMA patients starting at a very young age. In time they can hold their heads up, sit up unassisted, and some can even walk. Amazing! But for adults like myself who have lived with this disease for so many years? It is somewhat of a mystery how the drug will benefit us. Upon its release, many doctors claimed that Spinraza would not help adults with SMA type 1 whatsoever. Don't get your hopes up, they said. Easier said than done. Spinraza is also outrageously priced, amounting to $708,000 in the first year of treatment and $354,000 for every year thereafter. Why would the government or any hospital for that matter spend that money on challenging adults when they can be certain the drug will yield incredible results when given to infants? It is a very unfortunate yet logical decision to make in a world where the bottom dollar is most important, and empathy is nowhere to be found. My neurologist at Johns Hopkins denied me the treatment. I was devastated. I held myself together until we got back in the van to leave, then all my built-up hopes came pouring out through tears. Scripture tells us that God collects our tears. I am so thankful for that.

In late 2018, when I was still having mysterious stomach problems, my mom reached out to my childhood doctor to ask for help because we did not know where else to turn. In the conversation, Dr. Roy Proujansky asked if I was taking Spinraza and said he was going to consult one of his associates

Stewart / Broken / 59

Chapter 24

I was given a thorn in my flesh, a messenger of Satan, to torment me. Three times I pleaded with the Lord to take it away from me. But he said to me, "My grace is sufficient for you, for my power is made perfect in weakness." Therefore I will boast all the more gladly about my weaknesses, so that Christ's power may rest on me. That is why, for Christ's sake, I delight in weaknesses, in insults, in hardships, in persecutions, in difficulties. For when I am weak, then I am strong.

-   2 Corinthians 12:7-10

What kind of God would allow a mere shepherd boy to slay a giant who was easily twice his size for His glory? What kind of God would lay down His life in the worst way imaginable to save the very people cheering for his death? What kind of God would allow someone like me to be afflicted with disease, and deem that beautiful? To us mere mortals none of those things make sense. The truth is most people look at physical disabilities and see those people as being tragically disadvantaged – the underdogs. What if I told you that you are sorely mistaken? What if the truth is completely backwards than that which you might think?

The David in the story of David and Goliath was, by most accounts, at a disadvantage when he went into the Valley of Elah to do battle with the Philistine giant, Goliath. His brothers and other onlookers undoubtedly thought he was a lunatic. King Saul himself tried to reason with David, saying "You cannot go against this Philistine to do battle with him, for you are a lad and he is a man of war from his youth." David didn't care. He knew what nobody else did – that he was made for such a time as that. People today think it is crazy how David could kill a huge man weighted down with armor with one small stone, but he was not just a dumb kid who made a lucky shot. David was a Slinger: a special kind of warrior used in ancient armies. Slingers would place large rocks or heavy balls in a pouch and sling it around and around above their heads, gaining momentum with each turn until finally releasing it to demolish their target. It was an incredibly difficult skill to develop, and David was good at it. After all, he had to be in order to protect his sheep. We are talking about a guy who killed lions who messed with his flock like it was no big deal. David was many things, but a coward was not one of them. He won the battle because he trusted God wholeheartedly and he believed God had been preparing him for this specific moment his entire life up until that point. God uses underdogs all the time to do things that ordinary people won't, because they are afraid or do not want to tarnish their reputation or a number of other reasons.

The fact is there is a reason we are not all the same. I cannot minister to someone who is able-bodied and suffering from a drug addiction because I have no idea what that is like and thus, I would not be of any help. If you are an able-bodied person, you probably would not be able to minister to someone in my position because you do not know what it is like to be disabled. And that is alright. Certain people are more inclined to hear what you have to say because of who you are, while others are more apt to listen to whatever I have to say because of who I am. God has placed each of us on our own unique paths to allow us to be a blessing to different people in different ways. I am so thankful that God made me who I am because I have been able to help more people from a wheelchair than I ever could have done on two feet. Being the underdog is not a disadvantage; it is a strength. We must get past the way of thinking that some people are better than others based on their outward appearance. Survival of the fittest? Darwin denounced his own theory before he died. If anything, you should turn the tables entirely. Those who are viewed as being at a disadvantage usually have more perseverance and tenacity than regular people because they are constantly pushing themselves to be the best they can be. Nine times out of ten you will find that when "underdogs" are pushed to their breaking point, they strap on some wings and find that they can fly.

God loves the beaten and broken ones, and He promises to make everything beautiful in His time. He is famous for taking a mess and transforming it into a masterpiece. His philosophy when dealing with us mortals is completely backwards to that which we might think. He uses the weakest to move mountains and forever gives more grace. He is backwards, and He is good.

Chapter 25

I am constantly meeting people who cannot understand how I handle life in general. They're so amazed that I can actually function as a productive citizen. How do I eat? Just like you. I have a g-tube but can eat primarily by mouth with soft foods. I communicate by speaking, just like you. Both qualities of which are not typical for someone in my condition – but then again, very few live past the age of two anyway. I think it is pretty obvious I am anything but "normal". How do I go out? In my Cadillac of a wheelchair, which I drive completely unassisted with fiber optic laser controls. I like going to church, the movies, the mall, the nail salon, restaurants, and other fun places. I have a wheelchair accessible vehicle that my caregivers and I can use to go anywhere. I do my schoolwork and Candy Cane Kids work on my computer. I buy my own groceries, order prescriptions, and make phone calls from my computer as well. I do normal everyday tasks just as any able-bodied person does. The only difference is I may need some assistance getting there. I cannot take care of myself, but I know everything about my care and can tell people how to care for me. I do "projects", where I walk my caregivers through different artistic activities: cooking, gardening, making crafts – any creative activity I can find on Pinterest. One thing is for sure: I always keep my staff on their toes!

The fact that I am made differently than most does not stop me from loving life and chasing my God-given dreams. Growing up, I was never limited by my family, and it's the same today. There has never been anything I cannot do (except sky-diving – Mom vetoed that one). The word "can't" was never forced upon me. I might do something different than you, but I will get it done. I have learned to adapt to any circumstance, not saying "I can't" but "Let's figure out how I can". The greatest limitation anyone can have is within the mind. Some of the most disabled people have working bodies but do not use them because they have convinced themselves they cannot. Can't do anything right, can't have fun, can't go to college, can't get a job, can't have a family. Stop that thinking now. God gave you life for a reason. Quit wasting it and live it to the fullest, for all things are possible with Him. Look at me: I cannot move my head, but I will ride the Tower of Terror three times in a row. Don't accept less than the very best. Find a way to get it. I am still pushing the limits, always trying to excel and find new adventures. I refuse to be a vegetable in this life - God made me to move mountains.

I have not merely survived, but thrived, in this life from two things alone: God's abundant grace and mental strength. God gives grace to all, but it is up to you to decide to latch onto that gift of grace and run with it without stopping. Satan cannot ruin your life without your consent. God, in His goodness has given great power to the human mind; it is just that many let fear keep us from fulfilling our full potential. We are more than conquerors through Christ who conquered death and Hell.

Chapter 26

The year 2016 was a difficult year for me health wise, and 2017 unfortunately did not prove to be much better. In the year 2015, my feeding tube, which had not given me any issues in the 21 years I had had it, suddenly started causing major problems immediately following my obtaining a cellulitis infection on my entire torso. The cellulitis infection brought with it unimaginable pain, but after I started healing from that, a new intense pain presented itself in my stomach around my feeding tube. We kept thinking that the cellulitis had just gotten around the tube and just did not want to go away and kept trying to nurse it back to health. I tried every cream, powder, anything I could think of to help lessen the pain, but it only intensified the pain. Finally, I awoke and the pain I was experiencing around my g-tube was more excruciating than anything I had felt in a long time. Prescription pain medicine might as well have been breath mints, they did nothing. It was time to go to the hospital. Something was seriously wrong, and I could not go on any longer. The hour-long trip to John Hopkins Hospital felt like an eternity, and every bump in the road felt like someone pushing a knife deeper and deeper. At one point in time my sweet mother was literally driving ten miles per hours through the streets of Baltimore to keep me from crying out in agony. We finally arrived and checked into the Emergency Room. Maybe an hour and a half later I was given a bed in a small hospital room within the Emergency Department. Soon thereafter, hospital staff began conducting necessary measures to do tests to find the problem. The first educated guess was that I had a bowel obstruction, which I immediately shot down. Something else relating to my feeding tube is going on here. Keep trying. IV successfully placed, then I was sent to have a CAT scan with IV contrast. Three hours later a doctor pops by my room to tell us everything looked fine, and I should go home. I was devastated. I literally did not think I could make it home and back again. I cannot describe how emotional I was, how defeated I felt, how tired I was. Not even ten minutes later, another doctor came running in my room, saying that they were wrong, and I was not going anywhere. Another doctor had taken the time to take a second look at my scans and saw what the problem was: my g-tube had somehow gotten embedded in my abdominal wall. Left untreated much longer, I would have surely turned septic. I needed emergency surgery, but the surgeons could not get to me until the following evening. The next twenty-four hours consisted of me asking for IV pain medicine nonstop and fighting with ER nurses who would not help take me to the bathroom or give me my pain medicine. Mama Bear came out like never before to get me what I needed. And finally, the time came for me to have surgery where they pulled the feeding tube out of my abdominal wall and put it in the correct place in my stomach track. All was well and I was sent home to heal, which took me several months to do, but I did heal. For a year after that stomach surgery I had relatively no health problems. In May of 2016, exactly one year after my first g-tube displacement, that all-too-familiar pain came back. Well, at least I had made it a whole year before it messed up again. It could be worse. Let's just get it taken care of and move on. The date was set, the feeding tube was, again, taken out of my abdominal wall and put in the correct place, and I was good to go. Life was good. Until it happened again about a month later, and then again two months after that. For May of 2016 to May of 2017, my feeding tube came out place at least six times. It is impossible to determine the specific number of times it malfunctioned as it seemed it happened every few weeks. For several months in 2017 I did not feel right health wise. I could not pinpoint why but I truly felt that something was wrong. I am one of those skeptics who turns to online research in attempts to diagnose myself, because unfortunately I have had doctors blow me off several times. I had strange symptoms that I tried to focus on, but nothing added up. I was exhausted all the time and had horrible stomach pain. In September of 2017, things really took a turn for the worst. It began with me contracting respiratory MRSA – an acronym for methicillin resistant Staphylococcus aureus. MRSA is a "superbug" because it is a staph infection that is resistant to most antibiotics. MRSA can be deadly like me who is medically fragile if left untreated, but because it is antibiotic resistant it sometimes proves difficult to treat. I was on one, two, three different rounds of antibiotics that did not help before taking a more drastic approach to treatment. I went into John Hopkins Hospital, where I was given a PICC line

Chapter 27

The following are a few blog entries I wrote from late 2016 to late 2019:

I love when God speaks to me. I feel as though He does quite often. I feel I have a deep connection with Him, which makes sense to me considering all that He has brought me through.

I love to write. I have always been a writer. People complain about writing papers in school, but they are easier for me. I talk and people don't listen, don't understand. They dismiss me as being mentally handicapped and go on, not realizing I am intelligent and have something important to say. The frustration can be too much, so I stay quiet, smile, and nod. Writing, though, has given me a voice. I did not think I could share my thoughts at one point. I didn't know what I would have to say. It turns out I just had to listen for God's voice. He has given me a song to sing. It is amazing how I start typing with no idea what to write, and words begin to pour out of me without my knowledge of where they're even coming from. And it is in that time I know it is no one but God. For I am His messenger, as we all are.

We all have a voice. We are put on this earth to share our story and share the love of Jesus with others. If you are silent, you are wasting your God given potential to make a difference in this world. Maybe you can't speak fluently. Maybe you cannot write. Look at Moses: he needed an interpreter to lead the Israelites to the Promised Land. And through God he changed the course of History. God gave you a message to share with this world, so don't just keep it to yourself.

Except, what if you can't hear God's voice? This world is so loud, and His voice can be so soft. How do you know His voice? Or worse, what do you do when God is silent? Is He mad? Did you do something wrong? There is nothing more terrifying than fearing that God has forgotten you. Does He care? Can He even hear me screaming at the sky? Because life is hard, and I make mistakes. I have never been a skilled navigator (I get lost in the grocery store for crying out loud). But all I need is a whisper, a sign, something to let me know I am on the right track. My world can be out of control, I can be doing donuts like some crazy person trying to find whichever way is due North, when all I have to do is be still. Get somewhere quiet (shove in the headphones if need be) and wait. In such a fast-paced world that is not easy, but I can promise He is worth the wait! When the pain gets to be too much, wait. When you are unsure if you are doing the right thing, wait. And when the King of the universe speaks to you, you will know. That old saying, "the teacher is often silent when you're in the hardest test" might sound cliche, but it really is true. If you can hold on until the sky clears, you will hear the sweet voice of God and come out the other side better than you were before.

Life does not come with an instruction manual, but it does come with a God who loves us more than life itself and desires to have a relationship with us if only we can be silent to hear Him. Don't fear the silence, for it's in the silence that the Master's greatest creations are formed.

1 Kings 19:11-12: And, behold, the LORD passed by, and a great and strong wind rent the mountains, and brake in pieces the rocks before the LORD; but the LORD was not in the wind: and after the wind an earthquake; but the LORD was not in the earthquake: And after the earthquake a fire; but the LORD was not in the fire: and after the fire a still small voice.

To believe is to place one's trust in someone or something. You can believe in a being or place even if they cannot be seen by human eyes, though skeptics call this foolishness. Children believe in the Tooth Fairy and Easter Bunny. Some believe in parallel universes and extra-terrestrial beings. I believe in a God who came to earth several millennia ago just so He would understand my pain and die a horrendous death only to be resurrected so that today, here, and now, I could know Him. I am delusional, some say. "Whatever helps you deal with life", others say. I do not think I can ever explain the depth of my relationship with God, but it is not hard to believe in Him – it is not hard to love Him. To quote one of my favorite Christmas movies, The Santa Clause, "seeing isn't believing; believing is seeing." I have seen the hand of God at constant work in my life. Talk to any physician specializing in my diagnosis and they will tell you there is no medical answer as to how I am still alive and am the most functioning patient they have. Why is it that some (not all) terminal patients who believe in a higher power have a higher quality of life as well as a longer life expectancy? There are scientific studies on this, look it up. And I know what some are thinking: how can she love God in her condition? My question to that is, how can I not?

To believe in God is one thing. Many people, if asked, will say that they do believe in God. It is a whole other thing to believe that God is good; but take it one step further and choose to believe God is good to me. Or you. Because He is, and if we only open our eyes to see His unyielding grace, the act of believing is as easy as the act of breathing (says the girl on the ventilator. Anyway, you get the picture.). It is then obvious that God is faithful and in control of all. And in believing, we are given a sense of purpose and peace, even when trials come. Everything happens for a reason if you believe in a sovereign God.

The year 2017 was an exceedingly difficult one for me, filled with more pain than I can say. I thought 2016 was rough, but it was a cake walk compared to 2016, which was harder than the previous fifteen years combined from a medical perspective. Previously, I used to boast that I could handle anything, and Satan has sure enough put that to the test. I cried myself to sleep night after night from the pain. I did not understand the reason for that current storm, but I am certain that one day I will. Come Hell or high water I believe in the goodness of God and will persevere. I was facing yet another surgery at John Hopkins Medical Center to move my feeding tube to a different location in my stomach in hopes of relieving severe pain that I had been dealing with for several months. We had tried every other option, and nothing worked. Nevertheless, I still believed God will bring deliverance as He always has.

In a world where people refuse to believe that which they cannot see and do not value their fellow man, believing is a difficult practice to exercise. People are cruel and demeaning and enjoy crushing the spirit of believers, but the ones who remain steadfast in following Christ shall be rewarded in eternity. Life is hard but God is good, and He takes care of His children like the good father He is. Hold fast, dear one, for some day, you will look back on all God has brought you through and smile knowing there is no better place to be than in His will. Did God promise to never leave those who love Him? Did He promise to strengthen the weak? Did He promise to make you shine like the sun and hold you in the palm of His hand? Yes, He did. And if God said it, you can believe it.

I was sleeping so soundly, in that deep REM cycle that never quite hits until around 5am, regardless of what time I go to bed. Dreaming peacefully, when suddenly… What's that? Someone is grabbing my arm. Why? Must be 7:30: infusion time. But OWWW!! Feels like a piranha took a nibble out of my arm. They said it wouldn't hurt. They lied. Must roll onto back to relieve pressure. Then… Ugh, legs are killing me. More pillows. Arms aren't bent at a comfortable angle but be careful with the right ar- OOWWWWW!!!! That's it, no more moving. Sleep for a few hours. Get up, shower (my nemesis since I have to tape plastic wrap around my PICC line and we're back to the OOWWWWW ARE YOU KIDDING ME?!!), and throw pj's on with as little movement as possible. Done, hallelujah, now transfer into recliner. I'm not straight, but DON'T TOUCH MY ARM!!! Finally, comfortable. Feeling good! Oh… Never mind. Feel rough… Don't even know how… Just feel sick. Eat. More infusions. Sleep. Repeat. Of course, with my amazing family and some virtual coloring thrown in there, but yeah. This has been my life since last Thursday, when I had a PICC line placed to receive strong IV antibiotic infusions every twelve hours for two weeks because MRSA was making me extremely sick. Like, so sick. I do feel some better for sure, of which I am thankful. But I'm not better yet. Fighting this infection is ridiculously hard and has taken a toll on me physically. This is my current storm.

Storms are really quite beautiful if you take time to stop and watch. Truly a work of art, they are both terrifying and mesmerizing. I have been blessed with a living room full of windows, and sometimes on stormy days I will position my chair so I can watch. Many hate storms, and admittedly it is unpleasant to get drenched in a downpour, but what many do not know is the many benefits that accompany storms. First and most obvious, storms bring rain, which brings life and nourishment to all living plants and creatures. When lightning strikes it converts nitrogen gas into nitrogen compounds which fertilizes plant soil. Storms also rid the world of impurities and pollution. Storms heal.

While they can be destructive and scary at times, storms are necessary for growth of all forms of life. Without storms nothing grows and production of every kind ceases. And it is evident that life is meant to change. One thing always remains true: storms, regardless of how bad they are, never last forever. They may last a day, a week, even months, but eventually the rain will cease, and the sun will shine; and sometimes, if you are looking hard enough, you will even see a rainbow. And in that moment, everything was worth it.

I love the story found in Mark 4, and I've been thinking about it a lot lately. Jesus and His disciples were out on a boat and a bad storm arose, and it was so destructive that the waves were beginning to sink the ship. Everyone was terrified that they were going to die; that is, everyone except Jesus. He was in the bottom of the ship taking a nice nap. Everyone rushed to wake Him up, shouting things like "how can You be sleeping at a time like this? We are all going to die! Don't You care?" The Master went up on deck and with only one word spoken – "Peace" – the waves settled, and the sky cleared. The storm left with Christ's instruction. Afterwards, He turned to everyone and said, "Why don't you have any faith?" Jesus was not afraid of the storm because He knew His father had everything under control, and He could rest in that. The problem is, we humans tend to be extremely negative creatures, scared like sheep at any sign of distress. We know our Father loves us, but we are so used to being let down by people in this imperfect world that we doubt He will always come through. But He always does. Even when things seem bad, the Father is in control, using storms to bring healing and growth. We can trust our God, even when the wind and waves won't stop, and we are tired of fighting. He knows what He's doing, and the sun will shine again.

You might not understand this storm I am going through, and that is OK. I might not understand what you are going through and that's OK. God knows how hard the storms of life can be, and if only we can trust in His plan, and trust that He will not let the waves overtake us, we can learn to sleep in the storm.

There's something that's been on my mind more than usual as of late: the word "no". For such a small word, it packs quite a punch when uttered in conversation. NO, you can't do that. NO, you're wrong. NO, I won't help you. God created the word "no" for a specific purpose: to protect and to teach. Unfortunately, as with everything else originally designed for good, Satan took that word and twisted it into something that can be used to hurt, belittle, and show carelessness. What was meant for good is now often attributed with bad and sad instances fueled by anger or misunderstanding. And so here we are in the year 2018, where everyone is so fearful to utter the word "no" and offend anyone that our society has been turned upside down. Don't tell a little boy he's a boy because you might hurt his feelings (let's not even look at the studies showing how doing this can have serious long-term psychological repercussions, but anyway…). Don't stay in when that guy you like is at a party. Don't you deserve a good time? Don't correct your children for doing wrong… Lighten up! They're just being kids! Don't you want to be their friend?

In a word, NO.

It's not OK to do something simply because most people are doing the same thing. It's not OK to allow your kids to disrespect authority and act out of lawlessness. And it is so not OK to teach children that biology is irrelevant, and they can be their own God. No. I'm sorry if think it's right, but no.

Sometimes saying no would spare people much heartache.

We even play the yes game with a holy God.

If He loves me, He won't let me suffer.

Right. Let's not even look at how most of the original disciples of Christ suffered cruel deaths (did anyone actually find Paul's head once he was decapitated? That would certainly make for an interesting Resurrection story!), but anyway…

You don't understand. Jesus said in John 14:14, "If ye shall ask any thing in my name, I will do it." So, God can't say no!

This isn't Aladdin, and God is not a genie.

God is good and just and sometimes has a better plan than we do.

God can, and does, use the word no, but never without cause. And never does it not cause Him pain to do so.

Last night my stomach started hurting terribly bad, again. Today it began bleeding, again. I don't understand why this viscous cycle is still ongoing. If I'm being completely transparent, there are still days I feel I don't deserve to carry the constant weight that is Spinal Muscular Atrophy. But I believe in God's plan. In John 9, Christ and His disciples came upon a blind man. Scripture goes on to say, "And his disciples asked him, saying, Master, who did sin, this man, or his parents, that he was born blind? Jesus answered, Neither hath this man sinned, nor his parents: but that the works of God should be made manifest in him."

Do you understand?

On this roller-coaster ride of life, there are ups and downs, smiles and tears, joy and pain; all for His glory.

I might, someday, get some cure for SMA. I might not. Even so, God is still my everything. My four-year-old niece went swimming with her sister and "Abbi" (grandma) yesterday. I said in passing that I wished I could go with them. Haven so matter-of-factually spoke up and said "oh, Sissy, don't worry! You're going to walk one of these days! I even drew a picture of you walking! Want to see? We're going to swim in Heaven, and it will be SO FUN!!!" Out of the mouths of babes…

Even when God says no, He is still on His throne. Trust Him.

I remember coming out of one of the many surgeries I had on my stomach sometime in January of 2017, when the pain was so consuming that I could think of nothing whatsoever other than the searing pain. Every nerve was on fire. This must be what Hell is like. I am burning from the inside out but don't see smoke. I can't see anything. *Open your eyes.* The room is too bright. *What do I do? Where is Mom? I am going to die. God, please help me. God, please help me. GOD, I NEED YOU NOW!* And so, I speak. I cannot think, can't form sentences. In the fire God gives me two words and I push them out with any strength I have left: first a whisper, then louder.

"Help me."

Again.

"Help me."

Fight, Amber.

"Somebody help me!"

KEEP FIGHTING!

"Help me. Help me. Help me!"

My sweet Momma is over me. "It's alright, honey. You just came out of surger--"

"HELP ME! HELP ME! HELP ME! HELP ME! HELP ME! HELP ME! HELP M--"

"Amber, look at me. Look at me!"

There she is.

Just for good measure, I repeat my new anthem about ten more times.

I hear them speaking – first Mom, then Dad.

"Someone, please call the doctor. Nurse, can you please give her more medicine? She is in so much pain."

"I'll have to check. We can't give her much more…"

Meanwhile, I'm still screaming because that's all I know to do.

Then my mother cradles my face in her hands and does something only she can do… She calms me.

"They're getting more medicine. You already had a lot. You need to slow your breathing. Look at me. I know it hurts, but we're going to get through this,"

And so we did. Medicine did not bring much relief and I cried most of the night, but she was right beside me, dozing, holding me, and ringing for the nurse every hour for medication. My mother is my hero, my absolute best friend in life. I will never be able to thank God enough for giving me her, but I will try.

I am a thinker in case you have not noticed yet. My mind is constantly jumping from one topic to another, rarely pausing to rest in between. My thoughts keep me up at night unless I muzzle them with medications. Lately I've been thinking a lot about the human heart. The human body and organs are truly an amazing work of art. Did you know the heart pumps 2,000 gallons of blood through our bodies each day we are alive? It is vital for life, yet it only weighs 7-15 ounces. It beats around 100,000 times a day, usually in perfect synchrony. The human heart begins beating only four weeks post conception. And some say all this just happened by chance? Think about that.

In one hospital stay in early 2018, I suffered from a very sudden "minor" heart attack, according to physicians. Since being admitted, my blood pressure was scary low – so much so that I could not get any pain medicine for fear I would crash. Later the second night of my stay, my nurse was instructed to administer epinephrine – a drug given to help raise blood pressure to a stable number. We discovered very quickly that I am allergic to epinephrine. One second, I am carrying on with my mother and a visiting friend from church, the next I am feeling like I was hit by a freight train. I looked at my sweet mother: "Mom, help! It's my heart." Looked over at my monitors and everything was crashing – my heart rate, my blood pressure, this was bad. Mom runs out in the hallway screaming for help, and so many people came rushing in. Doctors, nurses, technicians, respiratory therapists… I had a large ICU room, and it was full of staff. "Amber, are you OK?" "Amber, I need you to talk to me." "Amber, tell me how you feel." Asking all kinds of questions, all while barking orders to the others to administer meds, stop others, and put in an arterial line to monitor my heart rate and blood pressure on a second by second basis. I looked at my mom, my best friend, and she is sobbing. She thought this was the end too. Everyone did. Dad and my pastor came immediately. I just can't bear to see her so scared, so I did all I could do; "Mom! Look at me! Keep your eyes on me. I'm OK. I'm going to be OK." Over and over and over I said those words while deep down I'm screaming "PLEASE DON'T TAKE ME HERE!! I'm not finished, and I can't leave my family!" It is quite a surreal thing to have one foot in this world and one foot in the next, and still making the choice to stay down here and keep pressing on. It is easy to quit, but it is more rewarding to stay and fight. It took a while and felt even longer, but eventually they got me stabilized, and there was peace.

Like the heart, the human brain is just as much of an incredible organ – so incredible in fact that the most renowned scientists have only begun to scratch the surface in understanding all the phenomenal abilities it possesses. The average person has around 70,000 thoughts per day. Contrary to popular belief, we use our entire brains rather than parts of it. The brain uses 20% of the total oxygen in the human body, and when awake generates enough energy to power a light bulb. There are more brain neurons and neuron connections than there are stars in the entire universe. The brain processes information at an approximate speed of 268 miles per hours. You get the picture; the human brain is another amazing creation of God.

In a perfect world, the heart would always function perfectly, there would be no need for modern medicine, and the human brain would be absolutely limitless. Unfortunately, Thanks to Adam and Eve and the entry of sin into this world, we suffer from pain, sickness, disease, and other tragedies that God never meant for us to endure. However, in His goodness, God can take what Satan means for evil and use it for good if we trust Him.

My cousin suffered a brain aneurysm and massive stroke at the age of seventeen, just a few weeks after I came home from that particular ICU stay. He was a senior in high school at the time who dedicated his life to sharing the message of hope through Jesus Christ. His chance of survival was next to nothing when he was brought in, but God has much bigger plans for Ricky, and through this trial God is being glorified and Ricky has learned to lean on God in a way he never had to before, making Him a true warrior and giving Him a very special relationship with his Heavenly Father that only some of us have the privilege of knowing. Ricky has helped more people through his battle than he would have had God spared him from the pain.

The point I am trying to make here is that life is very fragile and can change literally in the blink of an eye. One minute everything is great; the next you get T-boned on your way to work, or disease enters your body, or your heart stops beating… And your life is changed forever. Are you ready to face the uncertainties of this life? Because in one blink everything can change. "On Christ the solid rock I stand, all other ground is sinking sand" is true and I can testify to it. When the ground shatters beneath you, hold onto the hand of God and He will carry you through. It will not be easy, and it might not even end the way anyone wants, but I promise that going through Hell with God is much better than going it alone. Be prepared, friends. Take it from someone Satan loves to mess with: he can destroy your body and wreak havoc upon your mind, but if you have put your faith in Christ, at the end of it all you can still sing…

"When peace like a river attendeth my way

When sorrows like sea billows roll

Whatever my lot, Thou hast taught me to say

It is well, it is well with my soul."

Perhaps my favorite aspect of the Christian faith is that God pushes us to be resilient for Him. I think that some of the best parts of my life thus far have derived from times when I could not imagine going on another minute and I heard God whisper "keep pushing!" If you genuinely love the Lord, I feel you must build up a spirit of tenacity to counterbalance Satan's never-ending schemes. Maybe the old Devil doesn't bother you that much, but we go round and round on the daily. The battle has evolved into a dance of sorts: guessing his next move and stepping accordingly. I don't always dance well and get knocked down quite frequently, but I get back up every time. "Float like a butterfly, sting like a bee." Christ did not call us to surrender at the first sign of trouble. God gave us brains, but we fail to use them to find solutions when we face obstacles. We humans are notorious for believing our circumstances cannot get any worse when in actuality we can make them better through determination and a positive outlook. Life is what you make it.

In Mark 2 (and Matthew 9 and Luke 5 for that matter) we read about a quadriplegic man who had great friends that wouldn't give up on him when I assure you, he had given up on himself. For you see, Jesus was in Capernaum preaching. Imagine you desperately need a judicial pardon and the president just happens to come to your town for one day only. You would sacrifice everything just to have a chance to talk to him.

Tonight, when you lie in bed trying to go to sleep, do me a favor and lie completely still. Don't move one muscle, do not scratch one itch. It is hard. Living in a body that does not work is not for the faint of heart, and we can assume from scriptures that this man had lived a relatively long life in a disabled state. I can testify as an incredibly medically fragile individual that without the hope of Christ life is very bleak. This unnamed man did not know Jesus yet but had heard stories of this Messiah who could remove sin and restore sight to the blind. He had four friends and nothing to lose. His friends probably woke him up that morning, cleaned him up, loaded him up on a gurney, and headed out for an adventure! But alas, Christ was not preaching in a large synagogue, but a very small, non-ADA house. The crowd was crazy, everyone shoving to get a better view. They did not care that he was crippled, he was just in the way. What if it was cold and/or rainy? Even worse. Time to pack it up and go home. They had tried and failed. Here is where the story gets good: the group buckled down – all five of them – and decided they would not accept defeat that day. In what well may have taken hours, the four able-bodied men hoisted their friend to the roof and, as if they weren't tired enough, dug a gurney-sized hole in the roof of this very small house Jesus was preaching in and lowered him into the house because it was worth everything if Christ could help their friend. This certainly was not an easy task for this disabled man either, for he had to trust his four brothers to literally deliver his life safely into the hands of Jesus. The best part? His faith made him whole. "(Jesus said) 'I say unto thee, Arise, and take up thy bed, and go thy way into thine house.' And immediately he arose, took up the bed, and went forth before them all; insomuch that they were all amazed, and glorified God, saying, We never saw it on this fashion."

God likes to show off. God likes to use weak people to show His strength. God likes when we stand tall in the middle of a hurricane proclaiming, "God has brought me this far and will not leave me now!" God appreciates and awards our resilience. And it is worth every tear to have the King of the universe in your corner. With that you can move mountains and face every Goliath that comes your way.

It's OK if you have been knocked down a thousand times. Now is the time to rise.

Chapter 28

Ever look back in life and remember the sheer awfulness of different periods of time? The year 2018 consisted of everything nightmares are made of. I wrote the following excerpt in August of that year:

Someone lost their mother this morning. Someone just lost their sibling to drug overdose. I guarantee that several people have died today alone in car accidents across the nation. Someone is hooked up to a chemotherapy infusion, reading a book and praying for healing. A child somewhere is dying from Spinal Muscular Atrophy because their body just is not strong enough to keep fighting. Tragedies happen around us every day; yet who among us has actually stopped to see them and offer a shoulder to cry on?

I have SMA type 1. This is the worst kind of SMA one can have. I have had it my whole life. My prognosis was two years or less. I have beat every odd, expiration date, and stereotype thrown my way. Doctors do not understand. I am now one of the oldest patients with this disease and the most functioning one they have seen. I have come through so many battles; through nights where there was no logical reason I should have. I have had my deceased sister read me stories as a child. I've seen angels. I have visited Heaven. I talk to God, but He talks to me more.

You would think, "what else can come my way?" Right? I have overcome every trial. I'm unstoppable!

How naive I was...

I have been very sick over the past year; honestly two years, but the last year has been much worse than the first. I have had respiratory MRSA, serious feeding tube complications, was hospitalized for over a month on and off, and had cellulitis multiple times. I also broke my arm. You would think that's enough, right? It just keeps coming.

Even after we finally got the feeding tube complications seemingly fixed (buried bumper syndrome is not my friend), I have still been having stomach issues: random pain and nausea. I have been telling doctors that something was not right, but they were not listening. I finally sat down with a GI specialist last month after I was blown off yet again. "I mean no disrespect, but something is wrong - I know in my heart - and nobody is listening to me. The last time this happened, I got septic and almost died (early this year). If you won't help me, I will go somewhere else where they will. What will it be?" Next thing I know, I've got an IV in, they are drawing labs for a full blood panel, then doing a CT with IV and stomach contrast. Then we waited. And waited...

They scheduled an appointment with another specialist, but we couldn't get in for two weeks, which ended up being this past Friday. It was at a different location which was odd, but I didn't think anything of it. Mom and Dad both came with me to this appointment which does not usually happen, but I was happy, nonetheless. I assumed maybe we would talk about my diet since I switched to eating specific foods easily digestible for those with stomach disorders. I figured, what other tests could they want? I had genuinely tried to prepare myself. In my mind, the worst thing they could tell me is that my body does not process food and I can only have formula. This would be devastating, as eating is very enjoyable for me. But, if that was what the worst scenario was, I could handle it.

I wasn't ready for this...

"You have a mass on your liver"...

"It has to be removed"...

"We don't think it's cancerous, but it could be"...

"It could rupture"...

"With your feeding tube it's harder. We'll cut here and here"......

"Surgery is major with your condition and the ventilator"......

"4-6-hour long surgery".......

"About a week, at least, in the hospital"........

"Long recovery time"......

"We don't want to wait too long"......

"September"......

What?

This isn't real. It can't be.

I have SMA. Not a tumor.

I have enough to deal with. I can't have anything else.

I keep thinking I will wake up soon and it'll just be a crazy dream.

And yet, this is real.

We are looking into a different way to remove the mass. Please pray.

I don't understand.

It's not fair.

I am scared.

But I still love the Lord.

I will conquer this mountain just as I have the rest.

Provide for those who grieve in Zion—

to bestow on them a crown of beauty

instead of ashes,

the oil of joy

instead of mourning,

and a garment of praise

instead of a spirit of despair.

They will be called oaks of righteousness,

a planting of the Lord

for the display of his splendor. - Isaiah 61:3

I still have flashbacks from that time in life. Some feelings cannot be erased from the mind. A mass on my liver was the last thing I ever imagined would come my way. John Hopkins Medical Center was the hospital that oversaw me for everything else, so naturally they would have been the one to handle that particular issue also. Except for the fact that they only gave me one option and that was not really an option for me. The doctor assigned to me was arrogant and unwilling to think outside of the box to treat me. Imagine how it felt to find out so suddenly that you have a large mass on your liver which could be cancerous, only to meet a doctor with no bedside manner telling me I have no choice but to agree to a major liver resection surgery. If you're not sure what that entails, it's just what it sounds like: they remove an entire section of the liver along with the tumor. Very scary. As mentioned above, the surgery itself would be four to six hours long and incredibly risky. I had been so sick that entire year and was suffering from so much pain every day. I wasn't healthy in any aspect, though it wasn't my fault. We had to face the very real possibility that I might not be strong enough to live through such a drastic surgery. "Isn't there any other option?" The physician before me insisted there was not. Its times like that in which I am extra grateful for parents who have my best interest at heart. You see, I was completely numb at that point. In my eyes, life was over, I knew I would not make it through the operation. Oh, the irony of life! I had outlived spinal Muscular Atrophy type 1, And this is what would take me from this world? My parents went searching for another option. It was at that time that God brought Dr. Nabeel M. Akhter in my life, and I am so glad He did. Dr. Akhter specializes in Diagnostic Radiology and Nuclear Medicine at the University of Maryland Medical Center, and my mother found him online. God basically moved mountains just to get me in to see this wonderful doctor who is everything opposite of the last one. He was kind, gentle, and knew we could find a safer way to remove the tumor. He did just that: in early November of 2018, Dr. Akhter put me to sleep after many, many tests were done, and inserted a tiny catheter in my wrist and wove it all the way down to my liver. Once there, he deposited several small pellets into the tumor on my liver in order to cut off the blood supply. He also did a biopsy and found that the mass was not cancerous. Over time the tumor has gotten much smaller and is no longer a concern. To God be the glory.

Chapter 29

In the year 2019, I discovered a Godsend for my pain and stomach complications in the form of a leaf grown in Asia. It goes by the name Kratom, and it has brought more relief than most narcotics. Kratom is a member of the coffee family and is a natural opioid that interacts with the pain receptors. There is a long list of incredible benefits for this leaf, from opioid withdraw to relieving stomach problems from relaxing the smooth muscles. It helps with anxiety, nerve pain, boosts energy and focus, and more. Obviously, the government does not appreciate Kratom for the blessing it is because they are not profiting from it. Kratom is not FDA approved yet in this year 2020, and because of that, this medication is affordable. Additionally, that means that one must be wise in where they purchase it and how they dose it. I measure out my particular dose using a kitchen scale. I am now completely off all narcotic prescription drugs and feel better than I have in years. Anyone with chronic pain would greatly benefit from Red Vein Kratom, but not without conducting their own research and taking responsibly.

That same year, my family was approached by an organization known as the Center for Special Children: a tiny Amish built house/hospital in Strasburg PA (also known as the middle of nowhere) with a specific purpose of helping children and adults like myself with rare genetic conditions get access to the care they deserve. Evidently, neurological diseases are commonly found in Amish and Mennonite communities due to how close-knit relations are. Previously neither my family nor anyone I know had ever heard of this place because it was in such a remote location. I was offered the opportunity of a lifetime: a clinical trial for a special spinal port which would allow me to safely partake in receiving Spinraza treatment injections for the remainder of my life. Better yet, Biogen, the manufacturer of the Spinraza treatment injections for Spinal Muscular Atrophy, offered to cover 100% of the injection costs for the rest of my life also. Let us break down the numbers: during the first year of treatment, the patient must undergo a series of four loading doses. Those four doses alone cost $750,000. After that first year, the patient must have one injection each year for their entire lives thereafter. The cost of each dose is $375,000. My own neurologist looked me in the eyes years ago and told me that because of how old I am the medication was a gamble and infants respond so much better and it might not even help me and all I heard in that moment was "you're not worth it." That hurt me in ways no one will ever understand. But thank God Biogen does not think that. Unfortunately, the initial surgery to insert the spinal port for administering the treatment was postponed during that whole Coronavirus pandemic, but I still had hope that maybe I could have some gains from this treatment. We waited and waited. This other oral medication came out and we hoped I could get that instead, since it is much safer. Finally, one night in early August, we got the news I never wanted to hear: the risk of receiving Spinraza and contracting spinal meningitis does not outweigh the benefits which would be minimal at best. I was shattered. I went through a short period of mourning after that, for all that could have been. There is now a new safer treatment that just came out called Risdiplam, and we submitted all the paperwork requesting Medicaid to cover it. Literally less than one week before publishing this book, Mom got the call that my insurance had approved me to take Risdiplam. Excitement does not even begin to describe the feeling in that moment. I have high hopes that this treatment will give me some small gains such as strength and more energy, but ultimately, I am content regardless of what that has in store. There is ultimately one thing I am certain of: I have helped more people on four wheels than I ever could have on two legs. Regardless of what God continues to do in and through me, I will still love and serve Him with everything in me. He has been so good to me. I have a wonderful life. I love these words penned by Paul in Philippians 4: "I have learned to be content whatever the circumstances. I know what it is to be in need, and I know what it is to have plenty. I have learned the secret of being content in any and every situation, whether well fed or hungry, whether living in plenty or in want. I can do all this through him who gives me strength."

Chapter 30

 Second to having a personal relationship with Jesus Christ, the love and support of my amazing family has kept me functioning and thriving in life. I was never treated different than anyone else because I am not. If you have not figured that out by now, go back to Chapter 1. I have periods of extreme sickness, but outside of that, I am fully capable of achieving things that you can. I create beautiful art. I get groceries and make delicious meals. I provide multitudes of children with Christmas gifts and the Gospel of Jesus via website all from my computer and some elves who do the wrapping. I am a productive citizen who is deeply passionate about life. I have four college degrees that I worked hard for because no one ever told me I couldn't. My family has always been my biggest fans and as such they push me more than anyone else because they see all my potential. They push me when I don't want to take that next step. When all I see is pain, they remind me of who I am. My brother teases me relentlessly, but you don't know he beat up a boy on the playground back in the day because he made fun of me, and he'd probably do some adult version of that again if he had to. You do not know that he wanted to be my date for senior prom because he was so proud of how far I'd come. You don't know that he is a special brother unless you really know him. I am a proud aunt to three coolest kids in the world: Haven, Sage, and Ian. You know what is so awesome about being their aunt? I am not different in their eyes. I am not scary or weird. I am just their Aunt Sissy, who can figure out how to get them to listen and stay with me on our nature walks like anyone else. Once, I even tried the *don't make me come up there* bit when they wouldn't sleep. It worked! The point is, even though my family might look quite different in your eyes, to us it is just life. It's like I always say, *just keep rolling with it.* If people stare, stare right back! Dad taught me that. Of course, now days we just say "it's not polite to stare" or roll my eyes and make the ventilator alarm. That's always fun. I learned not to care what people who don't even know me think of me from a young age, because if I let that bother me, I would never venture outside of my house. I learned to (mostly) always stay kind and courageous from my parents. I learned to stand up for what you believe in because God made us to be warriors, not pacifists. I learned unconditional love and sacrifice from my mother who has not left me by myself in a hospital for 29 years and will sleep at the foot of my bed on the hardest nights. God first, family second, everything falls into place.

Stewart / Broken / 87

Chapter 31

I love how people think I just lay around all day every day without a care in the world. Granted, I do not have a regular job despite the fact that I have four college degrees and skill sets. Nevertheless, my life is nonstop because my mind is constantly running. From coordinating my care with the help of my mother, making sure that I have everything I need. Ordering medications and fighting for medical supplies. Trying to earn money through my art or freelance writing or freelance anything. Trying to be available for anyone who might need a friend or someone to talk to. I always have some crazy project I am working on. Always moving forward to the next opportunity, always making sure I do as much as I can to take care of myself. Did I forget that doctor's appointment? I have a meeting with my case manager next week, Mom. I forgot to email the doctor about that medication I found that might help me. I ordered grocery delivery for 4pm tomorrow. We need to call these places to see about getting a grant for Graduate school. My fish needs new water! Let's load up in the van and get some. Then there are days when I feel so bad it is all I can do to get out of bed for the day. Other days are especially difficult, and nothing seems to go right, and people I love often take the brunt of my frustration. Some days I crank the music up and just sing my heart out. A lesson everyone should learn is to never judge a person's worth based on their outward appearance. You would be surprised what the most physically disabled individuals can achieve when pushed to their greatest potential.

Chapter 32

Change is hard. The year 2020 was one of the most difficult years of my life, mentally and physically. My brother's family moved away around the same time the Coronavirus pandemic surprised us all. Everyone has their own ideas about the impact of COVID-19, but however you feel about it, the fact is that if someone like me contracts this virus it can very easily turn lethal. The fear can overwhelm you if you allow it to. Even after full state lockdowns in Maryland, it has not really been safe for me to venture out unless it is outside and no one else is around. Stress levels skyrocketed in my parents who want to protect me as best as they can in this new world full of unknowns. However, in spite of such scary times, God gave us peace. He shows Himself in a million different things if we only stop to see them. First, we saw an angel standing guard over my apartment level. Then I kept seeing this beautiful owl in my back yard, moving slightly closer to me each time I saw it. Finally, one evening in early Fall it flew right up to me glass doors before it was dark and stood there simply staring at me through the glass. I quickly asked my caregiver to turn my head so I could see it, and for a few moments we just sat looking at each other. Then it turned and flew away. Many people hold different philosophies regarding owls, but many of my friends, including my dear Pastor Harold Phillips, believe that the owl was a protector spirit or angel sent my way to comfort me during what ended up being a very tumultuous year filled with one infection after another and isolation to protect my health.

I love music. I can be having a really hard day, but when I blast my music on the television or through my headphones, I have peace. If I had the strength, I'd be a Gospel singer. However, God gave that gift to my sweet Daddy and he has the lungs to boot! One of my favorite songs is *God of the Storm* by This Hope. The message is simple: trust the Master of the rain to carry you through the storms that come your way. If ever that message fit the dreaded year that was 2020, that was it.

Chapter 33

People have difficulty understanding anything that is different because we as humans have a tendency to follow and appreciate that which we see as normal. We like everything looking nice and shiny. If something in life can't be wrapped up pretty with a big bow on it, nobody wants it. People avoid difficulty like the plague. We want a nice life, free from tragedy. Easy. Then you come across someone like me; I will not fit into any of your cookie cutter boxes. You can't plop some lipstick on me and simply ignore the fact that I am different. And that is OK. I am scarred and flawed and have been shattered time and time again. My life is crazy and chaotic and very messy, but also rewarding and filled with love. A real life is filled with laughter and pain, highs and lows. In what you might think of as pitiful or sad or not normal enough, there lies beauty and strength that is never found in living a normal life. The truth is everybody has something they struggle with. The difference between you and me is I show off my scars loud and proud because they have made me who I am. I am laying everything on the line here, broken for all to see. It is up to you to look deeper and find the beauty beyond that. Satan wants nothing more than for you to judge circumstances as too hard or too depressing and simply give up. To not find beauty in the ashes that lay before you. Push past that first layer and be surprised at what amazing things God has to show you beyond that. For any evil that exists in this world, there is a multitude of goodness that can be found if you search enough.

I have given you a glimpse of my life. I hope that it has shown you what happens when grace wins. I took the broken pieces of my life and gave them to a loving God, who in turn has given me an amazing life full of joy. In a world where people constantly doubt the existence of God, He is everything to me. He gave me life, and an amazing one at that. He has taken what was meant for evil and made a masterpiece out of it. Some people are destined to be healthy and strong, and live ordinary lives because that is how God can use them. And others are appointed to live different, difficult lives, because through that others see Jesus. Charles Spurgeon once said, "whenever God means to make a man great, He always breaks him in pieces first." I believe that is true, and I am certain that He is not finished with me yet. I am excited to see all that the future holds. My life has not always been easy, but I would not change any of it for anything. I love my life and every single part of the journey. Life is hard but God is good, and I would rather hold His hand through this life than walk alone for one day.

Do You Know Jesus?

Thank you for reading my book! I hope you have enjoyed my story. It is not over. I hope you have been inspired. More than anything, though, I hope that you have come to the realization that life is better with Jesus by your side. Perhaps your life is going great and you have told yourself that you will wait until you are older to meet Jesus, because you want to enjoy life and not feel guilty. We are not promised tomorrow. Do not risk your eternal destination for fleeting earthly pleasure. It is not worth it. The ball will drop in some way: a terminal diagnosis, financial trouble, relationship struggles, depression. Life has a way of knocking the wind out of you when you least expect it. Maybe you are going through a trial now and you feel like nobody truly understands what you're going through. Christ died for you. He understands you, and He loves you more than you can imagine. That is why he came to earth, lived a sinless life, died on a cross and resurrected three days later. He knows that we all have sin and have fallen short of the glory of God. We could never make ourselves good enough to be acceptable to God. He knows that and He loves us anyway. If you believe in Jesus' death and resurrection and ask Him to come into your heart and forgive your sins, He will accept you into the family of God and give you eternal life. It is really that simple. Knowing God is about so much more than having everlasting life, though. It is about having someone to help guide you through the rollercoasters of life. It is about being a part of something much bigger than yourself. It is about never having to walk through this life alone. It's beautiful and powerful and worth surrendering everything for. It is love. The love of God can wipe away any sin and restore the life that is broken. All you have to do is ask.

John 3:16-17 – For God so loved the world that He gave His only begotten son, that whosoever believeth in Him should not perish, but have everlasting life. For God sent not his Son into the world to condemn the world; but that the world through him might be saved.

Made in the USA
Middletown, DE
31 May 2021